THE PENGUIN SH
EDITED FROM THE O
BY G. B. HARRISON
B 29
THE LIFE OF TIMON OF ATHENS

WILLIAM SHAKESPEARE

The Life of
Timon of Athens

PENGUIN BOOKS

Penguin Books Ltd, Harmondsworth, Middlesex

CANADA: Penguin Books (Canada) Ltd, 178 Norseman Street,
Toronto 18, Ontario

AUSTRALIA: Penguin Books Pty Ltd, 762 Whitehorse Road,
Mitcham, Victoria

SOUTH AFRICA: Penguin Books (S.A.) Pty Ltd, Gibraltar House,
Regent Road, Sea Point, Cape Town

—

This edition first published 1956

The Editor gratefully acknowledges
the kindness of Dr J. C. Adams in
allowing the Penguin Shakespeare to
reproduce an engraving of his
model of the stage of the
Globe Playhouse

The portraits on the cover and on the title page
were engraved by Reynolds Stone

—

Made and printed in Great Britain
by Wyman & Sons Ltd, London, Fakenham and Reading

CONTENTS

THE WORKS OF SHAKESPEARE

PLAYS

APPROXIMATE DATE		FIRST PRINTED
Before 1594	HENRY VI *three parts*	*Folio* 1623
	RICHARD III	1597
	TITUS ANDRONICUS	1594
	LOVE'S LABOUR'S LOST	1598
	THE TWO GENTLEMEN OF VERONA	*Folio*
	THE COMEDY OF ERRORS	*Folio*
	THE TAMING OF THE SHREW	*Folio*
1594–1597	ROMEO AND JULIET (*pirated* 1597)	1599
	A MIDSUMMER NIGHT'S DREAM	1600
	RICHARD II	1597
	KING JOHN	*Folio*
	THE MERCHANT OF VENICE	1600
1597–1600	HENRY IV *part i*	1598
	HENRY IV *part ii*	1600
	HENRY V (*pirated* 1600)	*Folio*
	MUCH ADO ABOUT NOTHING	1600
	MERRY WIVES OF WINDSOR (*pirated* 1602)	*Folio*
	AS YOU LIKE IT	*Folio*
	JULIUS CÆSAR	*Folio*
	TROYLUS AND CRESSIDA	1609
1601–1608	HAMLET (*pirated* 1603)	1604
	TWELFTH NIGHT	*Folio*
	MEASURE FOR MEASURE	*Folio*
	ALL'S WELL THAT ENDS WELL	*Folio*
	OTHELLO	1622
	LEAR	1608
	MACBETH	*Folio*
	TIMON OF ATHENS	*Folio*
	ANTONY AND CLEOPATRA	*Folio*
	CORIOLANUS	*Folio*
After 1608	PERICLES (*omitted from the Folio*)	1609
	CYMBELINE	*Folio*
	THE WINTER'S TALE	*Folio*
	THE TEMPEST	*Folio*
	HENRY VIII	*Folio*

POEMS

DATES UNKNOWN		
	VENUS AND ADONIS	1593
	THE RAPE OF LUCRECE	1594
	SONNETS } A LOVER'S COMPLAINT }	1609
	THE PHŒNIX AND THE TURTLE	1601

WILLIAM SHAKESPEARE

William Shakespeare was born at Stratford upon Avon in April, 1564. He was the third child, and eldest son, of John Shakespeare and Mary Arden. His father was one of the most prosperous men of Stratford, who held in turn the chief offices in the town. His mother was of gentle birth, the daughter of Robert Arden of Wilmcote. In December, 1582, Shakespeare married Ann Hathaway, daughter of a farmer of Shottery, near Stratford; their first child Susanna was baptized on May 6, 1583, and twins, Hamnet and Judith, on February 22, 1585. Little is known of Shakespeare's early life; but it is unlikely that a writer who dramatized such an incomparable range and variety of human kinds and experiences should have spent his early manhood entirely in placid pursuits in a country town. There is one tradition, not universally accepted, that he fled from Stratford because he was in trouble for deer stealing, and had fallen foul of Sir Thomas Lucy, the local magnate; another that he was for some time a schoolmaster.

From 1592 onwards the records are much fuller. In March, 1592, the Lord Strange's players produced a new play at the Rose Theatre called *Harry the Sixth*, which was very successful, and was probably the *First Part of Henry VI*. In the autumn of 1592 Robert Greene, the best known of the professional writers, as he was dying wrote a letter to three fellow writers in which he warned them against the ingratitude of players in general, and in particular against an 'upstart crow' who 'supposes he is as much able to bombast out a blank verse as the best of you: and being an absolute Johannes Factotum is in his own conceit the only

Shake-scene in a country'. This is the first reference to Shakespeare, and the whole passage suggests that Shakespeare had become suddenly famous as a playwright. At this time Shakespeare was brought into touch with Edward Alleyne the great tragedian, and Christopher Marlowe, whose thundering parts of Tamburlaine, the Jew of Malta, and Dr Faustus Alleyne was acting, as well as Hieronimo, the hero of Kyd's *Spanish Tragedy*, the most famous of all Elizabethan plays.

In April, 1593, Shakespeare published his poem *Venus and Adonis,* which was dedicated to the young Earl of Southampton: it was a great and lasting success, and was reprinted nine times in the next few years. In May, 1594, his second poem, *The Rape of Lucrece,* was also dedicated to Southampton.

There was little playing in 1593, for the theatres were shut during a severe outbreak of the plague; but in the autumn of 1594, when the plague ceased, the playing companies were reorganized, and Shakespeare became a sharer in the Lord Chamberlain's company who went to play in the Theatre in Shoreditch. During these months Marlowe and Kyd had died. Shakespeare was thus for a time without a rival. He had already written the three parts of *Henry VI, Richard III, Titus Andronicus, The Two Gentlemen of Verona, Love's Labour's Lost, The Comedy of Errors,* and *The Taming of the Shrew.* Soon afterwards he wrote the first of his greater plays – *Romeo and Juliet* – and he followed this success in the next three years with *A Midsummer Night's Dream, Richard II,* and *The Merchant of Venice.* The two parts of *Henry IV,* introducing Falstaff, the most popular of all his comic characters, were written in 1597–8.

The company left the Theatre in 1597 owing to disputes over a renewal of the ground lease, and went to play at the

Curtain in the same neighbourhood. The disputes continued throughout 1598, and at Christmas the players settled the matter by demolishing the old Theatre and re-erecting a new playhouse on the South bank of the Thames, near Southwark Cathedral. This playhouse was named the Globe. The expenses of the new building were shared by the chief members of the Company, including Shakespeare, who was now a man of some means. In 1596 he had bought New Place, a large house in the centre of Stratford, for £60, and through his father purchased a coat-of-arms from the Heralds, which was the official recognition that he and his family were gentlefolk.

By the summer of 1598 Shakespeare was recognized as the greatest of English dramatists. Booksellers were printing his more popular plays, at times even in pirated or stolen versions, and he received a remarkable tribute from a young writer named Francis Meres, in his book *Palladis Tamia*. In a long catalogue of English authors Meres gave Shakespeare more prominence than any other writer, and mentioned by name twelve of his plays.

Shortly before the Globe was opened, Shakespeare had completed the cycle of plays dealing with the whole story of the Wars of the Roses with *Henry V*. It was followed by *As You Like It*, and *Julius Caesar*, the first of the maturer tragedies. In the next three years he wrote *Troylus and Cressida*, *The Merry Wives of Windsor*, *Hamlet*, and *Twelfth Night*.

On March 24, 1603, Queen Elizabeth I died. The company had often performed before her, but they found her successor a far more enthusiastic patron. One of the first acts of King James was to take over the company and to promote them to be his own servants, so that henceforward they were known as the King's Men. They acted now very frequently at Court, and prospered accordingly. In the early years of the reign Shakespeare wrote the more sombre comedies, *All's Well that Ends Well,* and *Measure for Measure,* which were followed by *Othello, Macbeth,* and *King Lear.* Then he returned to Roman themes with *Antony and Cleopatra* and *Coriolanus.*

Since 1601 Shakespeare had been writing less, and there were now a number of rival dramatists who were introducing new styles of drama, particularly Ben Jonson (whose first successful comedy, *Every Man in his Humour,* was acted by Shakespeare's company in 1598), Chapman, Dekker, Marston, and Beaumont and Fletcher who began to write in 1607. In 1608 the King's Men acquired a second playhouse, an indoor private theatre in the fashionable quarter of the Blackfriars. At private theatres, plays were performed indoors; the prices charged were higher than in the public playhouses, and the audience consequently was more select. Shakespeare seems to have retired from the stage about this time: his name does not occur in the various lists of players after 1607. Henceforward he lived for the most part at Stratford, where he was regarded as one of the most important citizens. He still wrote a few plays, and he tried his hand at the new form of tragi-comedy – a play with tragic incidents but a happy ending – which Beaumont and Fletcher had popularized. He wrote four of these – *Pericles, Cymbeline, The Winter's Tale,* and *The Tempest,* which was acted at Court in 1611. For the last four years of his life he lived in retirement. His son Hamnet had died in 1596: his two daughters were now married. Shakespeare died at Stratford upon Avon on April 23, 1616, and was buried in the chancel of the church, before the high altar. Shortly afterwards a memorial which still exists, with a portrait bust, was set up on the North wall. His wife survived him.

When Shakespeare died fourteen of his plays had been separately published in Quarto booklets. In 1623 his surviving fellow actors, John Heming and Henry Condell, with the co-operation of a number of printers, published a collected edition of thirty-six plays in one Folio volume, with an engraved portrait, memorial verses by Ben Jonson and others, and an Epistle to the Reader in which Heming and Condell make the interesting note that Shakespeare's 'hand and mind went together, and what he thought, he uttered with that easiness that we have scarce received from him a blot in his papers'.

The plays as printed in the Quartos or the Folio differ considerably from the usual modern text. They are often not divided into scenes, and sometimes not even into acts. Nor are there place-headings at the beginning of each scene, because in the Elizabethan theatre there was no scenery. They are carelessly printed and the spelling is erratic.

THE ELIZABETHAN THEATRE

Although plays of one sort and another had been acted for many generations, no permanent playhouse was erected in England until 1576. In the 1570s the Lord Mayor and Aldermen of the City of London and the players were constantly at variance. As a result James Burbage, then the leader of the great Earl of Leicester's players, decided that he would erect a playhouse outside the jurisdiction of the Lord Mayor, where the players would no longer be hindered by the authorities. Accordingly in 1576 he built the Theatre in Shoreditch, at that time a suburb of London. The experiment was successful, and by 1592 there were two more playhouses in London, the Curtain (also in Shore-ditch), and the Rose on the south bank of the river, near Southwark Cathedral.

Elizabethan players were accustomed to act on a variety of stages; in the great hall of a nobleman's house, or one of the Queen's palaces, in town halls and in yards, as well as their own theatre.

The public playhouse for which most of Shakespeare's plays were written was a small and intimate affair. The outside measurement of the Fortune Theatre, which was built in 1600 to rival the new Globe, was but eighty feet square. Playhouses were usually circular or octagonal, with three tiers of galleries looking down upon the yard or pit, which was open to the sky. The stage jutted out into the yard so that the actors came forward into the midst of their audience.

Over the stage there was a roof, and on either side doors by which the characters entered or disappeared. Over the back of the stage ran a gallery or upper stage, with windows on either side, which was used whenever an upper scene was needed, as when Romeo climbs up to Juliet's bedroom, or the citizens of Angiers address King John from the walls. The space beneath this upper stage was known as the tiring house; it was concealed from the audience by a curtain which would be drawn back to reveal an inner stage, for such scenes as the witches' cave in *Macbeth*, Prospero's cell, or Juliet's tomb.

There was no general curtain concealing the whole stage, so that all scenes on the main stage began with an entrance and ended with an exit. Thus in tragedies the dead must be carried away. There was no scenery, and therefore no limit to the number of scenes, for a scene came to an end when the characters left the stage. When it was necessary for the

THE GLOBE THEATRE
Wood-engraving by R. J. Beedham after a reconstruction by J. C. Adams

exact locality of a scene to be known, then Shakespeare indicated it in the dialogue; otherwise a simple property or a garment was sufficient; a chair or stool showed an indoor scene, a man wearing riding boots was a messenger, a king wearing armour was on the battlefield, or the like. Such simplicity was on the whole an advantage; the spectator was not distracted by the setting and Shakespeare was able to use as many scenes as he wished. The action passed by very quickly: a play of 2500 lines of verse could be acted in two hours. Moreover, since the actor was so close to his audience, the slightest subtlety of voice and gesture was easily appreciated.

The company was a 'Fellowship of Players', who were all partners and sharers. There were usually ten to fifteen full members, with three or four boys, and some paid servants. Shakespeare had therefore to write for his team. The chief actor in the company was Richard Burbage, who first distinguished himself as Richard III; for him Shakespeare wrote his great tragic parts. An important member of the company was the clown or low comedian. From 1594 to 1600 the company's clown was Will Kemp; he was succeeded by Robert Armin. No women were allowed to appear on the stage, and all women's parts were taken by boys.

THE LIFE OF TIMON OF
ATHENS

Timon of Athens was first printed in the First Folio in 1623, where it was included – apparently as an afterthought – among the Tragedies, between *Romeo and Juliet* and *Julius Caesar*. It had at first been intended that *Troylus and Cressida* should follow *Romeo and Juliet*, but for some reason *Troylus and Cressida* was removed, leaving a gap of thirty pages between the last page of *Romeo and Juliet*, numbered 79, and the first page of *Julius Caesar*, numbered 109. *Timon*, however, is eight pages shorter than *Troylus and Cressida*, and so the pagination of the Folio was considerably disturbed; the pages of *Timon* are numbered 80, 81, 82, 81, 82, 83, and thence consecutively to 98. There seems therefore to have been some understandable hesitation on the part of the original editors of the First Folio whether to include or omit *Timon of Athens*.

The text of *Timon* is peculiar. At times the play runs smoothly, with all the speeches well written and the action consistent; but at other times the diction breaks down into a confused medley of prose, blank verse, rhymed verse, free verse and mere doodling. This unevenness is less obvious in the 'accepted' text which was freely re-aligned and tidied by editors of the eighteenth and nineteenth centuries. A good example of the unevenness will be found in the passage where the Steward laments Timon's extravagances – P. 42 L. 8 – P. 43. L. 4. In the Penguin text the arrangement of the Folio is followed; previous editors rearrange as follows:

FLAVIUS: *Aside.* What will this come to?
He commands us to provide and give great gifts,
And all out of an empty coffer.
Nor will he know his purse, or yield me this:
To show him what a beggar his heart is,
Being of no power to make his wishes good.
His promises fly so far beyond his state
That what he speaks is all in debt, he owes
For every word. He is so kind that he now
Pays interest for 't. His land's put to their books.
Well, would I were gently put out of office
Before I were forced out!
Happier is he that has no friend to feed
Than such that do e'en enemies exceed.
I bleed inwardly for my lord.   [*Exit.*]

TIMON: You do yourselves
Much wrong; you hate too much your own merits.
Here, my lord, a trifle of our love.

2 LORD: With more than common thanks I will receive it.

3 LORD: Oh, he's the very soul of bounty!

TIMON: And now I remember, my lord, you gave
Good words the other day of a bay courser
I rode on. 'Tis yours, because you liked it.

3 LORD: Oh, I beseech you, pardon me, my lord, in that.

TIMON: You may take my word, my lord, I know no man
Can justly praise but what he does affect.
I weigh my friend's affection with mine own.
I'll tell you true. I'll call to you.

Various explanations have been offered of the peculi-
arities of the diction, such as revision of Shakespeare's work
by another, or revision of another's work by Shakespeare,
or inept cutting of the play for performance. The likeliest

guess is that of E. K. Chambers*, that *Timon of Athens* is a
first version of a play that Shakespeare never finished. The
passage noted, and many others, are just the kind of first
draft that comes when an author's inspiration is flagging or
when he is tired or bored with what he is writing.

There is no external fact, contemporary mention, or
quotation by which the date of *Timon* can be checked, but
the style is unmistakably that of Shakespeare's later period
when he wrote *Lear* or *Coriolanus* (1606–1609). There was
at this time a theatrical fashion for melancholic and misan-
thropic characters who rail on the world in extravagant and
bitter language. Several of the most striking passages in
Timon can be paralleled in the plays of other writers or even
of Shakespeare himself, as if he was imitating or borrowing
from others or from himself. Thus Timon's mighty curses
on Athens and on mankind (P. 71 L. 30, P. 72 L. 15) are an
echo of Coriolanus's curse on Rome when he is banished,
or a kind of re-writing of the mad speeches of Lear.

The direct source of the play is a casual anecdote in
North's Plutarch, in the Life of Marcus Antonius, which
Shakespeare had already twice used – in the writing of
Iulius Caesar and of *Antony and Cleopatra* :

> Antonius, he forsook the city and company of his
> friends, and built him a house by the sea by the isle of
> Pharos, upon certain forced mounts which he caused to
> be cast into the sea, and dwelt there as a man that ban-
> ished himself from all men's company, saying he would
> lead Timon's life, because he had the like wrong offered
> him, that was before offered unto Timon; and that for
> the unthankfulness of those he had done good unto, and

**William Shakespeare* : A Study of Facts and Problems, 1930,
i, 482.

whom he took to be his friends, he was angry with all
men and would trust to no man. This Timon was a
citizen of Athens, that lived about the war of Pelopon-
nesus, as appeareth by Plato and Aristophanes' comedies;
in the which they mocked him, calling him a viper and
malicious man unto mankind, to shun all other men's
companies but the company of young Alcibiades, a bold
and insolent youth, whom he would greatly feast and
make much of, and kissed him very gladly. Apemantus
wondering at it, asked him the cause why he meant to
make so much of that young man alone, and to hate all
others. Timon answered him: 'I do it,' he said, 'because I know that one day he shall do great mischief unto
the Athenians.' This Timon would sometimes have
Apemantus in his company, because he was much like of
his nature and conditions, and also followed him in
manner of life. On a time when they solemnly celebrated
the feast called *Choæ* at Athens (to wit, the feasts of the
dead where they make sprinklings and sacrifices for the
dead) and that they two then feasted together by themselves, Apemantus said unto the other: 'Oh, here is a
trim banquet, Timon!' Timon answered again: 'Yea,'
said he, 'so thou wert not here.' It is reported of him
also, that this Timon on a time (the people having
assembled in the market place about the despatch of
some affairs) got up into the pulpit of orations, where the
other orators commonly use to speak unto the people;
and silence being made, every man listening to what he
would say, because it was a wonder to see him in that
place, at length he began to speak in this manner: 'My
lords of Athens, I have a little yard at my house where
there groweth a fig tree, on the which many citizens
have hanged themselves; and because I mean to make

some building on that place, I thought it good to let you all understand it, that before that the fig tree be cut down, if any of you be desperate, you may there in time go hang yourselves.' He died in the city of Hales, and was buried upon the seaside. Now it chanced so, that the sea getting in, it compassed his tomb round about, that no man could come to it; and upon the same was written this epitaph:

Here lies a wretched corse, of wretched soul bereft:
Seek not my name: a plague consume you wicked
  wretches left!

It is reported that Timon himself, when he lived, wrote this epitaph; for that which is commonly rehearsed was not his, but made by the poet Callimachus:

Here lie I, Timon, who alive all living men did hate:
Pass by and curse thy fill: but pass, and stay not here
  thy gait.

Many other things we could tell you of this Timon, but this little shall suffice at this present.

From Plutarch's Life of Alcibiades Shakespeare could also have gathered some interesting details, but he seems to have taken little except the general impression that Alcibiades was a young gentleman who turned against his native city of Athens.

The story of Timon occurs also in one of the *Dialogues* of the second-century Greek writer Lucian. In this version Timon appeals to the god Zeus to drop his thunderbolts on those ingrates who have taken his wealth and turn on him now that he is no more than a poor farm labourer. Zeus is at last moved by Timon's prayers, and orders Hermes, the messenger of the gods, to take Riches to Timon; but Riches demurs because Timon had treated him so badly in the past, and a long argument follows on the right use of wealth. But at last Riches agrees to go with Hermes. They find Timon digging; his companions now are Poverty, Toil, Endurance, Wisdom and Manliness. Timon greets Hermes and Riches rudely; but when persuaded that Riches is a gift from Zeus he reluctantly relents, with the remark that they are bringing him ill luck because he is most happy in his poverty, and with renewed wealth he will again be full of cares. Timon discovers a treasure, and thereupon resolves to buy the farm where he is working, but to keep his new wealth to himself. Almost at once, his former parasites appear and gather round him – Gnathonides the toady, Philiades the flatterer, Demas the orator, and Thrasycles the philosopher, who preaches temperance best when drunk. Timon drives them all away.

There is little in this version – except the discovery of the treasure – to suggest that Shakespeare used it; the tone and the moral implications are quite different from those in the play.

In spite of the unevennesses of the diction, the copy used by the compositor for the Folio seems to have been good; there are a few difficulties of reading, but in general the text seems to have been carefully prepared. No divisions into Acts and scenes are noted in the Folio but the stage directions are full.

In the present edition, as with the other texts in the Penguin Shakespeares, the original version has been followed closely. Spellings have been modernized, the excessive use of capitals has been modified, but the punctuation, which marks how the lines are to be spoken, has been kept except in a few instances where it seemed obviously wrong.

The text will thus appear somewhat different to those who are accustomed to the 'accepted' text, but it is nearer to what Shakespeare wrote, and to that which the King's Men used at the Globe – if indeed they ever acted *Timon of Athens*.

The Life of
Timon of Athens

THE ACTORS' NAMES

TIMON of Athens
LUCIUS and
LUCULLUS, two Flattering Lords
APEMANTUS, a Churlish Philosopher
SEMPRONIUS, another Flattering Lord
ALCIBIADES, an Athenian Captain
POET
PAINTER
JEWELLER
MERCHANT
Certain Senators
Certain Maskers
Certain Thieves
FLAMINIUS, one of Timon's Servants
SERVILIUS, another
CAPHIS
VARRO
PHILO   Several Servants to Usurers
TITUS
LUCIUS
HORTENSIS
VENTIDIUS, one of Timon's false Friends
CUPID
SEMPRONIUS
With divers other Servants,
And Attendants

I. 1

Enter Poet, Painter, Jeweller, Merchant, and Mercer,
at several doors.

POET: Good day Sir.

PAINTER: I am glad y'are well.

POET: I have not seen you long, how goes the World?

PAINTER: It wears sir, as it grows.

POET: Ay that's well known:
But what particular rarity? What strange,
Which manifold record not matches: see
Magic of bounty, all these spirits thy power
Hath conjur'd to attend.
I know the Merchant.

PAINTER: I know them both: th'other's a Jeweller.

MERCHANT: O 'tis a worthy Lord.

JEWELLER: Nay that's most fix'd.

MERCHANT: A most incomparable man, breath'd as it were,
To an untireable and continuate goodness:
He passes.

JEWELLER: I have a jewel here.

MERCHANT: O pray lets see't. For the Lord Timon, sir?

JEWELLER: If he will touch the estimate. But for that –

POET: When we for recompence have prais'd the vile,
It stains the glory in that happy verse,
Which aptly sings the good.

MERCHANT: 'Tis a good form.

JEWELLER: And rich: here is a water look ye.

PAINTER: You are rapt sir, in some work, some Dedication
to the great Lord.

POET: A thing slipp'd idlely from me.
   Our poesy is as a gown, which uses
   From whence 'tis nourish'd: the fire i'th'flint
   Shows not, till it be struck: our gentle flame
   Provokes itself, and like the current flies
   Each bound it chafes. What have you there?
PAINTER: A picture sir: when comes your book forth?
POET: Upon the heels of my presentment sir.
   Let's see your piece.
PAINTER: 'Tis a good piece.
POET: So 'tis, this comes off well, and excellent.
PAINTER: Indifferent.
POET: Admirable: How this grace
   Speaks his own standing: what a mental power
   This eye shoots forth? How big imagination
   Moves in this lip, to th'dumbness of the gesture,
   One might interpret.
PAINTER: It is a pretty mocking of the life:
   Here is a touch: Is't good?
POET: I will say of it,
   It tutors Nature, artificial strife
   Lives in these touches, livelier than life.
                    Enter certain Senators.
PAINTER: How this Lord is followed.
POET: The Senators of Athens, happy men.
PAINTER: Look moe.
POET: You see this confluence, this great flood of visitors,
   I have in this rough work, shap'd out a man
   Whom this beneath world doth embrace and hug
   With amplest entertainment: My free drift
   Halts not particularly, but moves itself
   In a wide sea of wax, no levell'd malice
   Infects one comma in the course I hold,

But flies an eagle flight, bold, and forth on,
Leaving no tract behind.

PAINTER: How shall I understand you?

POET: I will unbolt to you.
You see how all conditions, how all minds,
As well of glib and slipp'ry creatures, as
Of grave and austere quality, tender down
Their services to Lord Timon: his large Fortune,
Upon his good and gracious Nature hanging,
Subdues and properties to his love and tendance
All sorts of hearts; yea, from the glass-fac'd flatterer
To Apemantus, that few things loves better
Than to abhor himself; even he drops down
The knee before him, and returns in peace
Most rich in Timon's nod.

PAINTER: I saw them speak together.

POET: Sir, I have upon a high and pleasant hill
Feign'd Fortune to be thron'd.
The base o'th'mount
Is rank'd with all deserts, all kind of natures
That labour on the bosom of this Sphere,
To propagate their states; among'st them all,
Whose eyes are on this Sovereign Lady fix'd,
One do I personate of Lord Timon's frame,
Whom Fortune with her ivory hand wafts to her,
Whose present grace, to present slaves and servants
Translates his rivals.

PAINTER: 'Tis conceiv'd, to scope
This throne, this fortune, and this hill methinks
With one man beckon'd from the rest below,
Bowing his head against the steepy Mount
To climb his happiness, would be well express'd
In our condition.

POET: Nay Sir, but hear me on:
  All those which were his fellows but of late,
  Some better than his value; on the moment
  Follow his strides, his lobbies fill with tendance,
  Rain sacrificial whisperings in his ear,
  Make sacred even his stirrup, and through him
  Drink the free air.

PAINTER: Ay marry, what of these?

POET: When Fortune in her shift and change of mood
  Spurns down her late beloved; all his dependents
  Which labour'd after him to the Mountain's top,
  Even on their knees and hand, let him sit down,
  Not one accompanying his declining foot.

PAINTER: Tis common:
  A thousand moral paintings I can show,
  That shall demonstrate these quick blows of Fortune's,
  More pregnantly than words. Yet you do well,
  To show Lord Timon, that mean eyes have seen
  The foot above the head.

Trumpets sound.
Enter Lord Timon, addressing himself courteously
to every Suitor.

TIMON: Imprison'd is he, say you?

MESSENGER: Ay my good Lord, five talents is his debt,
  His means most short, his creditors most strait:
  Your honourable letter he desires
  To those have shut him up, which failing,
  Periods his comfort.

TIMON: Noble Ventidius well:
  I am not of that feather, to shake off
  My friend when he must need me. I do know him
  A Gentleman, that well deserves a help,
  Which he shall have. I'll pay the debt, and free him.

MESSENGER: Your Lordship ever binds him.

TIMON: Commend me to him, I will send his ransom,
And being enfranchised bid him come to me;
'Tis not enough to help the feeble up,
But to support him after. Fare you well.

MESSENGER: All happiness to your Honour.

Exit.

Enter an old Athenian.

OLDMAN: Lord Timon, hear me speak.

TIMON: Freely good Father.

OLDMAN: Thou hast a servant nam'd Lucilius.

TIMON: I have so: What of him?

OLDMAN: Most noble Timon, call the man before thee.

TIMON: Attends he here, or no? Lucillius.

LUCILLIUS: Here at your Lordship's service.

OLDMAN: This fellow here, Lord Timon, this thy
By night frequents my house. I am a man   [creature,
That from my first have been inclin'd to thrift,
And my estate deserves an heir more rais'd,
Than one which holds a trencher.

TIMON: Well: what further?

OLDMAN: One only Daughter have I, no kin else,
On whom I may confer what I have got:
The Maid is fair, a'th'youngest for a bride,
And I have bred her at my dearest cost
In qualities of the best. This man of thine
Attempts her love: I prithee (noble Lord)
Join with me to forbid him her resort,
Myself have spoke in vain.

TIMON: The man is honest.

OLDMAN: Therefore he will be Timon.
His honesty rewards him in itself,
It must not bear my Daughter.

TIMON: Does she love him?

OLDMAN: She is young and apt:
   Our own precedent passions do instruct us
   What levity's in youth.

TIMON: Love you the Maid?

LUCILIUS: Ay my good Lord, and she accepts of it.

OLDMAN: If in her marriage my consent be missing,
   I call the Gods to witness, I will choose
   Mine heir from forth the beggars of the world,
   And dispossess her all.

TIMON: How shall she be endowed,
   If she be mated with an equal husband?

OLDMAN: Three Talents on the present; in future, all.

TIMON: This Gentleman of mine
   Hath serv'd me long:
   To build his fortune, I will strain a little,
   For 'tis a bond in men. Give him thy Daughter,
   What you bestow, in him I'll counterpoise,
   And make him weigh with her.

OLDMAN: Most noble Lord,
   Pawn me to this your Honour, she is his.

TIMON: My hand to thee,
   Mine Honour on my promise.

LUCILIUS: Humbly I thank your Lordship, never may
   That state or Fortune fall into my keeping,
   Which is not owed to you.
                              Exit.

POET: Vouchsafe my labour,
   And long live your Lordship.

TIMON: I thank you, you shall hear from me anon:
   Go not away. What have you there, my friend?

PAINTER: A piece of painting, which I do beseech
   Your Lordship to accept.

TIMON: Painting is welcome.
  The painting is almost the natural man:
  For since Dishonour traffics with man's nature,
  He is but outside: These pencill'd figures are
  Even such as they give out. I like your work,
  And you shall find I like it; Wait attendance
  Till you hear further from me.

PAINTER: The Gods preserve ye.

TIMON: Well fare you Gentleman: give me your hand.
  We must needs dine together: sir your jewel
  Hath suffered under-praise.

JEWELLER: What my Lord, dispraise?

TIMON: A mere satiety of commendations,
  If I should pay you for't as 'tis extoll'd,
  It would unclue me quite.

JEWELLER: My Lord, 'tis rated
  As those which sell would give: but you well know,
  Things of like value differing in the owners,
  Are prized by their masters. Believ't dear Lord,
  You mend the jewel by the wearing it.

TIMON: Well mock'd.

Enter Apemantus.

MERCHANT: No my good Lord, he speaks the common
    tongue
  Which all men speak with him.

TIMON: Look who comes here, will you be chid?

JEWELLER: We'll bear with your Lordship.

MERCHANT: He'll spare none.

TIMON: Good morrow to thee,
  Gentle Apemantus.

APEMANTUS: Till I be gentle, stay thou for thy good mor-
    row.
  When thou art Timon's dog, and these knaves honest.

TIMON: Why dost thou call them knaves, thou know'st them not?

APEMANTUS: Are they not Athenians?

TIMON: Yes.

APEMANTUS: Then I repent not.

JEWELLER: You know me, Apemantus?

APEMANTUS: Thou know'st I do, I call'd thee by thy name.

TIMON: Thou art proud Apemantus?

APEMANTUS: Of nothing so much, as that I am not like Timon.

TIMON: Whither art going?

APEMANTUS: To knock out an honest Athenian's brains.

TIMON: That's a deed thou'lt die for.

APEMANTUS: Right, if doing nothing be death by th'Law.

TIMON: How lik'st thou this picture Apemantus?

APEMANTUS: The best, for the innocence.

TIMON: Wrought he not well that painted it.

APEMANTUS: He wrought better that made the Painter, and yet he's but a filthy piece of work.

PAINTER: Y'are a dog.

APEMANTUS: Thy Mother's of my generation: what's she, if I be a dog?

TIMON: Wilt dine with me Apemantus?

APEMANTUS: No: I eat not Lords.

TIMON: And thou should'st, thou'dst anger Ladies.

APEMANTUS: O they eat Lords;
So they come by great bellies.

TIMON: That's a lascivious apprehension.

APEMANTUS: So, thou apprehend'st it,
Take it for thy labour.

TIMON: How dost thou like this jewel, Apemantus?

APEMANTUS: Not so well as plain-dealing, which will not cost a man a doit.

TIMON: What dost thou think 'tis worth?

APEMANTUS: Not worth my thinking.
How now Poet?

POET: How now Philosopher?

APEMANTUS: Thou liest.

POET: Art not one?

APEMANTUS: Yes.

POET: Then I lie not.

APEMANTUS: Art not a Poet?

POET: Yes.

APEMANTUS: Then thou liest:
Look in thy last work, where thou hast feign'd him a
worthy Fellow.

POET: That's not feign'd, he is so.

APEMANTUS: Yes he is worthy of thee, and to pay thee for
thy labour. He that loves to be flattered, is worthy o'th'
flatterer. Heavens, that I were a Lord.

TIMON: What would'st do then Apemantus?

APEMANTUS: E'en as Apemantus does now, hate a Lord
with my heart.

TIMON: What thyself?

APEMANTUS: Ay.

TIMON: Wherefore?

APEMANTUS: That I had no angry wit to be a Lord.
Art not thou a Merchant?

MERCHANT: Ay Apemantus.

APEMANTUS: Traffic confound thee, if the Gods will not.

MERCHANT: If traffic do it, the Gods do it.

APEMANTUS: Traffic's thy God, and thy God confound thee.
Trumpet sounds. Enter a Messenger.

TIMON: What trumpet's that?

MESSENGER: 'Tis Alcibiades, and some twenty Horse
All of Companionship.

B

TIMON: Pray entertain them, give them guide to us.
You must needs dine with me: go not you hence
Till I have thank'd you: when dinner's done
Show me this piece, I am joyful of your sights.

Enter Alcibiades with the rest.

Most welcome Sir.

APEMANTUS: So, so: their aches contract, and starve your
supple joints: that there should be small love amongst
these sweet knaves, and all this courtesy. The strain of
man's bred out into baboon and monkey.

ALCIBIADES: Sir, you have sav'd my longing, and I feed
Most hungerly on your sight.

TIMON: Right welcome Sir:
Ere we depart, we'll share a bounteous time
In different pleasures.
Pray you let us in.

Exeunt.

Enter two Lords.

1 LORD: What time a day is't Apemantus?

APEMANTUS: Time to be honest.

1 LORD: That time serves still.

APEMANTUS: The most accursed thou that still omit'st it.

2 LORD: Thou art going to Lord Timon's Feast.

APEMANTUS: Ay, to see meat fill knaves, and wine heat
fools.

2 LORD: Fare thee well, fare thee well.

APEMANTUS: Thou art a fool to bid me farewell twice.

2 LORD: Why Apemantus?

APEMANTUS: Should'st have kept one to thyself, for I
mean   to give thee none.

1 LORD: Hang thyself.

APEMANTUS: No I will do nothing at thy bidding:
Make thy requests to thy friend.

2 LORD: Away unpeaceable dog,
  Or I'll spurn thee hence.

APEMANTUS: I will fly like a dog, the heels a'th'ass.

1 LORD: He's opposite to humanity.
  Come shall we in,
  And taste Lord Timon's bounty: he outgoes
  The very heart of kindness.

2 LORD: He pours it out: Plutus the God of Gold
  Is but his Steward: no meed but he repays
  Seven-fold above itself: No gift to him,
  But breeds the giver a return: exceeding
  All use of quittance.

1 LORD: The noblest mind he carries,
  That ever govern'd man.

2 LORD: Long may he live in fortunes. Shall we in?
  I'll keep you company.

Exeunt.

I.2

Hoboyes playing loud music.
A great Banquet serv'd in: and then, Enter Lord Timon,
the States, the Athenian Lords, Ventidius which Timon
redeem'd from prison. Then comes dropping after all
Apemantus discontentedly like himself.

VENTIDIUS: Most honoured Timon,
  It hath pleas'd the Gods to remember my Father's age,
  And call him to long peace:
  He is gone happy, and has left me rich:
  Then, as in grateful virtue I am bound
  To your free heart, I do return those talents
  Doubled with thanks and service, from whose help
  I deriv'd liberty.

TIMON: O by no means,
Honest Ventidius: You mistake my love,
I gave it freely ever, and there's none
Can truly say he gives, if he receives:
If our betters play at that game, we must not dare
To imitate them: faults that are rich are fair.

VENTIDIUS: A noble spirit.

TIMON: Nay my Lords, ceremony was but devis'd at first
To set a gloss on faint deeds, hollow welcomes,
Recanting goodness, sorry ere 'tis shown:
But where there is true friendship, there needs none.
Pray sit, more welcome are ye to my fortunes,
Than my fortunes to me.

I LORD: My Lord, we always have confess'd it.

APEMANTUS: Ho ho, confess'd it? Hang'd it? Have you
not?

TIMON: O Apemantus, you are welcome.

APEMANTUS: No: You shall not make me welcome:
I come to have thee thrust me out of doors.

TIMON: Fie, th'art a churl, ye have got a humour there
Does not become a man, 'tis much to blame:
They say my Lords, *Ira furor brevis est,*
But yond man is very angry.
Go, let him have a table by himself:
For he does neither affect company,
Nor is he fit for't indeed.

APEMANTUS: Let me stay at thine apperil Timon,
I come to observe, I give thee warning on't.

TIMON: I take no heed of thee: Th'art an Athenian, therefore welcome: I myself would have no power, prithee
let my meat make thee silent.

APEMANTUS: I scorn thy meat, 'twould choke me: for I
should ne'er flatter thee. Oh you Gods! What a number

of men eats Timon, and he sees 'em not? It grieves me to
see so many dip their meat in one man's blood, and all
the madness is, he cheers them up too.
I wonder men dare trust themselves with men.
Me thinks they should invite them without knives,
Good for their meat, and safer for their lives.
There's much example for't, the fellow that sits next him,
now parts bread with him, pledges the breath of him in
a divided draught: is the readiest man to kill him. 'Tas
been proved, if I were a huge man I should fear to drink
at meals, lest they should spy my wind-pipe's dangerous
notes, great men should drink with harness on their
throats.

TIMON: My Lord in heart: and let the health go round.

2 LORD: Let it flow this way my good Lord.

APEMANTUS: Flow this way? A brave fellow. He keeps
his tides well, those healths will make thee and thy state
look ill, Timon.
Here's that which is too weak to be a sinner,
Honest water, which ne'er left man i'th'mire:
This and my food are equals, there's no odds,
Feasts are too proud to give thanks to the Gods.

Apemantus' Grace.

> *Immortal Gods, I crave no pelf,*
> *I pray for no man but myself,*
> *Grant I may never prove so fond,*
> *To trust man on his oath, or bond.*
> *Or a harlot for her weeping,*
> *Or a dog that seems asleeping,*
> *Or a keeper with my freedom,*
> *Or my friends if I should need 'em.*
> *Amen. So fall to't:*
> *Rich men sin, and I eat root.*

Much good dich thy good heart, Apemantus.

TIMON: Captain,

Alcibiades, your heart's in the field now.

ALCIBIADES: My heart is ever at your service, my Lord.

TIMON: You had rather be at a breakfast of enemies, than a dinner of friends.

ALCIBIADES: So they were bleeding new my Lord, there's no meat like'em, I could wish my best friend at such a feast.

APEMANTUS: Would all those flatterers were thine enemies then, that then thou might'st kill'em: and bid me to'em.

I LORD: Might we but have that happiness my Lord, that you would once use our hearts, whereby we might express some part of our zeals, we should think ourselves forever perfect.

TIMON: Oh no doubt my good Friends, but the Gods themselves have provided that I shall have much help from you: how had you been my Friends else. Why have you that charitable title from thousands? Did not you chiefly belong to my heart? I have told more of you to myself, than you can with modesty speak in your own behalf. And thus far I confirm you. Oh you Gods (think I,) what need we have any Friends; if we should ne'er have need of 'em? They were the most needless creatures living; should we ne'er have use for 'em? And would most resemble sweet instruments hung up in cases, that keeps their sounds to themselves. Why I have often wish'd myself poorer, that I might come nearer to you: we are born to do benefits. And what better or properer can we call our own, than the riches of our Friends? Oh what a precious comfort 'tis, to have so many like brothers commanding one another's fortunes. Oh joys, e'en made away ere't can be born : mine eyes cannot hold out water methinks, to forget their faults. I drink to you.

APEMANTUS: Thou weep'st to make them drink, Timon.

2 LORD: Joy had the like conception in our eyes.
And at that instant, like a babe sprung up.

APEMANTUS: Ho, ho : I laugh to think that babe a bastard.

3 LORD: I promise you my Lord you mov'd me much.

APEMANTUS: Much.

*Sound Tucket. Enter the Maskers of Amazons, with
lutes in their hands, dancing and playing.*

TIMON: What means that trump ? How now ?

Enter Servant.

SERVANT: Please you my Lord, there are certain Ladies
Most desirous of admittance.

TIMON: Ladies ? what are their wills ?

SERVANT: There comes with them a fore-runner my Lord,
which bears that office, to signify their pleasures.

TIMON: I pray let them be admitted.

Enter Cupid with the Mask of Ladies.

CUPID: Hail to thee worthy Timon and to all that of his
bounties taste : the five best senses acknowledge thee
their Patron, and come freely to gratulate thy plenteous
bosom.
There taste, touch all, pleas'd from thy table rise :
They only now come but to feast thine eyes.

TIMON: They're welcome all, let 'em have kind admittance. Music make their welcome.

LUCILIUS: You see my Lord, how ample y'are belov'd.

APEMANTUS: Hoyday,
What a sweep of vanity comes this way.
They dance ? They are madwomen,
Like madness is the glory of this life,

As this pomp shows to a little oil and root.
We make ourselves Fools, to disport ourselves,
And spend our flatteries, to drink those men,
Upon whose age we void it up again
With poisonous spite and envy.
Who lives, that's not depraved, or depraves;
Who dies, that bears not one spurn to their graves
Of their Friends' gift:
I should fear, those that dance before me now,
Would one day stamp upon me: 'Tas been done,
Men shut their doors against a setting Sun.

*The Lords rise from Table, with much adoring of
Timon, and to show their loves, each single out an Amazon,
and all dance, men with women, a lofty strain or two
to the hoboyes and cease.*

TIMON: You have done our pleasures
Much grace (fair Ladies)
Set a fair fashion on our entertainment,
Which was not half so beautiful, and kind:
You have added worth unto't, and lustre,
And entertain'd me with mine own device.
I am to thank you for't.

I LORD: My Lord you take us even at the best.

APEMANTUS: Faith for the worst is filthy, and would not
hold taking, I doubt me.

TIMON: Ladies, there is an idle banquet attends you,
Please you to dispose yourselves.

ALL LADIES: Most thankfully, my Lord.

Exeunt.

TIMON: Flavius.

FLAVIUS: My Lord.

TIMON: The little casket bring me hither.

FLAVIUS: Yes, my Lord. More jewels yet?

There is no crossing him in's humour,
Else I should tell him well, yfaith I should;
When all's spent, he'd be cross'd then, and he could:
'Tis pity Bounty had not eyes behind,
That man might ne're be wretched for his mind.

Exit.

1 LORD: Where be our men?

SERVANT: Here my Lord, in readiness.

2 LORD: Our horses.

TIMON: O my Friends:
I have one word to say to you: Look you, my good Lord
I must entreat you honour me so much,
As to advance this jewel, accept it, and wear it,
Kind my Lord.

1 LORD: I am so far already in your gifts.

ALL: So are we all.

Enter a Servant.

SERVANT: My Lord, there are certain Nobles of the Senate
newly alighted, and come to visit you.

TIMON: They are fairly welcome.

Enter Flavius.

FLAVIUS: I beseech your Honour, vouchsafe me a word, it
does concern you near.

TIMON: Near? why then another time I'll hear thee.
I prythee let's be provided to show them entertainment.

FLAVIUS: I scarce know how.

Enter another Servant.

SERVANT: May it please your Honour, Lord Lucius
(Out of his free love) hath presented to you
Four Milk-white horses, trapp'd in silver.

TIMON: I shall accept them fairly: let the presents
Be worthily entertain'd.

Enter a third Servant.

How now? What news?

3 SERVANT: Please you my Lord, that honourable
Gentleman Lord Lucullus, entreats your company tomorrow, to hunt with him, and ha's sent your Honour
two brace of greyhounds.

TIMON: I'll hunt with him,
And let them be receiv'd, not without fair reward.

FLAVIUS: What will this come to?
He commands us to provide, and give great gifts, and all
out of an empty coffer:
Nor will he know his purse, or yield me this,
To show him what a beggar his heart is,
Being of no power to make his wishes good.
His promises fly so beyond his state,
That what he speaks is all in debt, he owes for ev'ry
word:
He is so kind, that he now pays interest for't;
His land's put to their books. Well, would I were
Gently put out of office, before I were forc'd out:
Happier is he that has no friend to feed,
Than such that do e'en enemies exceed.
I bleed inwardly for my Lord.

Exit.

TIMON: You do yourselves much wrong,
You bate too much of your own merits.
Here my Lord, a trifle of our love.

2 LORD: With more than common thanks
I will receive it.

3 LORD: O he's the very soul of bounty.

TIMON: And now I remember my Lord, you gave good
words the other day of a bay courser I rode on. 'Tis yours
because you lik'd it.

1 LORD: Oh, I beseech you pardon me, my Lord, in that.

TIMON: You may take my word my Lord: I know no
man can justly praise, but what he does affect. I weigh my
Friend's affection with mine own: I'll tell you true, I'll
call to you.

ALL LORDS: O none so welcome.

TIMON: I take all, and your several visitations
So kind to heart, 'tis not enough to give:
Methinks, I could deal kingdoms to my Friends,
And ne'er be weary. Alcibiades,
Thou art a Soldier, therefore seldom rich,
It comes in charity to thee: for all thy living
Is mong'st the dead: and all the lands thou hast
Lie in a pitch'd field.

ALCIBIADES: Ay, defil'd land, my Lord.

1 LORD: We are so virtuously bound.

TIMON: And so am I to you.

2 LORD: So infinitely endear'd.

TIMON: All to you. Lights, more lights.

1 LORD: The best of happiness, honour, and fortunes
Keep with you Lord Timon.

TIMON: Ready for his Friends.

Exeunt Lords.

APEMANTUS: What a coil's here, serving of becks, and jut-
ting out of bums. I doubt whether their legs be worth the
sums that are given for 'em.
Friendship's full of dregs,
Methinks false hearts, should never have sound legs.
Thus honest Fools lay out their wealth on curtsies.

TIMON: Now Apemantus (if thou wert not sullen)
I would be good to thee.

APEMANTUS: No, I'll nothing; for if I should be brib'd
too, there would be none left to rail upon thee, and then
thou wouldst sin the faster. Thou giv'st so long Timon (I

fear me) thou wilt give away thyself in paper shortly.
What needs these feasts, pomps, and vain-glories?

TIMON: Nay, and you begin to rail on Society once, I am
sworn not to give regard to you. Farewell, and come with
better music.

Exit.

APEMANTUS: So: Thou wilt not hear me now, thou shalt
not then. I'll lock thy heaven from thee:
Oh that men's ears should be
To Counsel deaf, but not to Flattery.

Exit.

II. 1

Enter a Senator.

SENATOR: And late five thousand: to Varro and to Isidore
He owes nine thousand, besides my former sum,
Which makes it five and twenty. Still in motion
Of raging waste? It cannot hold, it will not.
If I want gold, steal but a beggar's dog,
And give it Timon, why the dog coins gold.
If I would sell my horse, and buy twenty more
Better than he; why give my horse to Timon.
Ask nothing, give it him, it foals me straight
And able horses: No Porter at his gate,
But rather one that smiles, and still invites
All that pass by. It cannot hold, no reason
Can sound his state in safety. Caphis hoa,
Caphis I say.

Enter Caphis.

CAPHIS: Here sir, what is your pleasure.

SENATOR: Get on your cloak, and haste you to Lord
Timon,

Importune him for my moneys, be not ceas'd
With slight denial; nor then silenc'd, when
Commend me to your Master, and the cap
Plays in the right hand, thus: but tell him,
My uses cry to me; I must serve my turn
Out of mine own, his days and times are past,
And my reliances on his fracted dates
Have smit my credit. I love, and honour him,
But must not break my back, to heal his finger.
Immediate are my needs, and my relief
Must not be toss'd and turn'd to me in words,
But find supply immediate. Get you gone,
Put on a most importunate aspect,
A visage of demand: for I do fear
When every feather sticks in his own wing,
Lord Timon will be left a naked gull,
Which flashes now a Phoenix, get you gone.

CAPHIS: I go sir.

SENATOR: I go sir?
Take the bonds along with you,
And have the dates in. Come.

CAPHIS: I will Sir.

SENATOR: Go.

Exeunt.

II.2

Enter Steward, with many bills in his hand.

STEWARD: No care, no stop, so senseless of expense,
That he will neither know how to maintain it,
Nor cease his flow of riot. Takes no account
How things go from him, nor resume no care
Of what is to continue: never mind,

Was to be so unwise, to be so kind.

What shall be done, he will not hear, till feel:

I must be round with him, now he comes from hunt-
ing.

Fie, fie, fie, fie.

Enter Caphis, Isidore, and Varro.

CAPHIS: Good even Varro: what, you come for money?

VARRO: Is't not your business too?

CAPHIS: It is, and yours too, Isidore?

ISIDORE: It is so.

CAPHIS: Would we were all discharg'd.

VARRO: I fear it.

CAPHIS: Here comes the Lord.

Enter Timon, and his Train.

TIMON: So soon as dinner's done, we'll forth again
My Alcibiades. With me, what is your will?

CAPHIS: My Lord, here is a note of certain dues.

TIMON: Dues? whence are you?

CAPHIS: Of Athens here, my Lord.

TIMON: Go to my Steward.

CAPHIS: Please it your Lordship, he hath put me off
To the succession of new days this month:
My Master is awak'd by great occasion,
To call upon his own, and humbly prays you,
That with your other noble parts, you'll suit,
In giving him his right.

TIMON: Mine honest Friend,
I prithee but repair to me next morning.

CAPHIS: Nay, good my Lord.

TIMON: Contain thyself, good Friend.

VARRO: One Varro's servant, my good Lord.

ISIDORE: From Isidore, he humbly prays your speedy payment.

CAPHIS: If you did know my Lord, my Master's wants.

VARRO: 'Twas due on forfeiture my Lord, six weeks, and
past.

ISIDORE: Your Steward puts me off my Lord, and I
Am sent expressly to your Lordship.

TIMON: Give me breath:
I do beseech you good my Lords keep on,
I'll wait upon you instantly. Come hither; pray you
How goes the world, that I am thus encounter'd
With clamorous demands of debt, broken bonds,
And the detention of long since due debts
Against my honour?

STEWARD: Please you Gentlemen,
The time is unagreeable to this business:
Your importunacy cease, till after dinner,
That I may make his Lordship understand
Wherefore you are not paid.

TIMON: Do so my Friend, see them well entertain'd.

STEWARD: Pray draw near.

Exit.

Enter Apemantus and Fool.

CAPHIS: Stay, stay, here comes the Fool with Apemantus,
let's ha' some sport with 'em.

VARRO: Hang him, he'll abuse us.

ISIDORE: A plague upon him dog.

VARRO: How dost Fool?

APEMANTUS: Dost dialogue with thy shadow?

VARRO: I speak not to thee.

APEMANTUS: No 'tis to thyself. Come away.

ISIDORE: There's the Fool hangs on your back already.

APEMANTUS: No thou stand'st single, th'art not on him
yet.

CAPHIS: Where's the Fool now?

APEMANTUS: He last ask'd the question. Poor rogues, and usurer's men, bawds between gold and want.

ALL: What are we Apemantus?

APEMANTUS: Asses.

ALL: Why?

APEMANTUS: That you ask me what you are, and do not know yourselves. Speak to 'em Fool.

FOOL: How do you Gentlemen?

ALL: Gramercies good Fool:

How does your Mistress?

FOOL: She's e'en setting on water to scald such chickens as you are. Would we could see you at Corinth.

APEMANTUS: Good, Gramercy.

Enter Page.

FOOL: Look you, here comes my Master's Page.

PAGE: Why how now Captain? what do you in this wise Company.

How dost thou Apemantus?

APEMANTUS: Would I had a rod in my mouth, that I might answer thee profitably.

PAGE: Prithee Apemantus read me the superscription of these letters, I know not which is which.

APEMANTUS: Canst not read?

PAGE: No.

APEMANTUS: There will little learning die then that day thou art hang'd. This is to Lord Timon, this to Alcibiades. Go thou was't born a bastard, and thou'lt die a bawd.

PAGE: Thou was't whelped a dog, and thou shalt famish a dog's death.

Answer not, I am gone.

Exit.

APEMANTUS: E'en so thou out-runst grace,

Fool I will go with you to Lord Timon's.

FOOL: Will you leave me there?

APEMANTUS: If Timon stay at home.

You three serve three usurers?

ALL: I would they serv'd us.

APEMANTUS: So would I:

As good a trick as ever hangman serv'd thief.

FOOL: Are you three usurers' men?

ALL: Ay Fool.

FOOL: I think no usurer, but has a fool to his servant. My Mistress is one, and I am her Fool: when men come to borrow of your Masters, they approach sadly, and go away merry: but they enter my Mistress's house merrily, and go away sadly. The reason of this?

VARRO: I could render one.

APEMANTUS: Do it then, that we may account thee a whoremaster, and a knave, which notwithstanding thou shalt be no less esteemed.

VARRO: What is a whoremaster Fool?

FOOL: A Fool in good clothes, and something like thee. 'Tis a spirit, sometime 't appears like a Lord, sometimes like a Lawyer, sometimes like a Philosopher, with two stones more than's artificial one. He is very often like a Knight; and generally, in all shapes that man goes up and down in, from fourscore to thirteen, this spirit walks in.

VARRO: Thou art not altogether a Fool.

FOOL: Nor thou altogether a wise man,

As much foolery as I have, so much wit thou lack'st.

APEMANTUS: That answer might have become Apemantus.

ALL: Aside, aside, here comes Lord Timon.

Enter Timon and Steward.

APEMANTUS: Come with me (Fool) come.

FOOL: I do not always follow lover, elder brother, and
   woman, sometimes the philosopher.
STEWARD: Pray you walk near,
   I'll speak with you anon.

Exeunt.

TIMON: You make me marvel wherefore ere this time
   Had you not fully laid my state before me,
   That I might so have rated my expense
   As I had leave of means.
STEWARD: You would not hear me:
   At many leisures I propos'd.
TIMON: Go to:
   Perchance some single vantages you took,
   When my indisposition put you back,
   And that unaptness made your minister
   Thus to excuse yourself.
STEWARD: O my good Lord,
   At many times I brought in my accompts,
   Laid them before you, you would throw them off,
   And say you found them in mine honesty,
   When for some trifling present you have bid me
   Return so much, I have shook my head, and wept:
   Yea 'gainst th'authority of manners, pray'd you
   To hold your hand more close: I did endure
   Not seldom, nor no slight checks, when I have
   Prompted you in the ebb of your estate,
   And your great flow of debts; my lov'd Lord,
   Though you hear now (too late) yet now's a time,
   The greatest of your having, lacks a half,
   To pay your present debts.
TIMON: Let all my land be sold.
STEWARD: 'Tis all engag'd, some forfeited and gone,
   And what remains will hardly stop the mouth

Of present dues; the future comes apace:
What shall defend the interim, and at length
How goes our reck'ning?

TIMON: To Lacedemon did my land extend.

STEWARD: O my good Lord, the world is but a word,
Were it all yours, to give it in a breath,
How quickly were it gone.

TIMON: You tell me true.

STEWARD: If you suspect my husbandry or falsehood,
Call me before th'exactest Auditors,
And set me on the proof. So the Gods bless me,
When all our offices have been oppress'd
With riotous feeders, when our vaults have wept
With drunken spilth of wine; when every room
Hath blaz'd with Lights, and bray'd with minstrelsy,
I have retir'd me to a wasteful cock,
And set mine eyes at flow.

TIMON: Prithee no more.

STEWARD: Heavens have I said, the bounty of this Lord;
How many prodigal bits have slaves and peasants
This night englutted: who is not Timon's,
What heart, head, sword, force, means, but is Lord
    Timon's:
Great Timon, noble, worthy, royal Timon:
Ah, when the means are gone, that buy this praise,
The breath is gone, whereof this praise is made:
Feast won, fast lost; one cloud of winter showers,
These flies are couch'd.

TIMON: Come sermon me no further.
No villainous bounty yet hath passed my heart;
Unwisely, not ignobly have I given.
Why dost thou weep, canst thou the conscience lack,
To think I shall lack friends: secure thy heart,

If I would broach the vessels of my love,
And try the argument of hearts, by borrowing,
Men, and men's fortunes could I frankly use
As I can bid thee speak.

STEWARD: Assurance bless your thoughts.

TIMON: And in some sort these wants of mine are crown'd,
That I account them blessings. For by these
Shall I try friends. You shall perceive
How you mistake my fortunes;
I am wealthy in my friends.
Within there, Flavius, Servilius?

Enter three Servants.

SERVILIUS: My Lord, my Lord.

TIMON: I will dispatch you severally.
You to Lord Lucius, to Lord Lucullus you, I hunted with
his Honour today; you to Sempronius; commend me to
their loves; and I am proud say, that my occasions have
found time to use 'em toward a supply of money: let the
request be fifty Talents.

FLAMINIUS: As you have said, my Lord.

STEWARD: Lord Lucius and Lucullus? Humh.

TIMON: Go you sir to the Senators;
Of whom, even to the State's best health; I have
Deserv'd this hearing: bid 'em send o'th'instant
A thousand Talents to me.

STEWARD: I have been bold
(For that I knew it the most general way)
To them, to use your signet, and your name,
But they do shake their heads, and I am here
No richer in return.

TIMON: Is't true? Can't be?

STEWARD: They answer in a joint and corporate voice,
That now they are at fall, want treasure, cannot

Do what they would, are sorry : you are honourable,
But yet they could have wish'd, they know not,
Something hath been amiss; a noble nature
May catch a wrench; would all were well; 'tis pity,
And so intending other serious matters,
After distasteful looks; and these hard fractions
With certain half-caps, and cold moving nods,
They froze me into silence.

TIMON: You Gods reward them :
Prithee man look cheerily. These old fellows
Have their ingratitude in them hereditary :
Their blood is cak'd, 'tis cold, it seldom flows,
'Tis lack of kindly warmth, they are not kind;
And Nature, as it grows again toward earth,
Is fashion'd for the journey, dull and heavy.
Go to Ventidius (prythee be not sad,
Thou art true, and honest; Ingeniously I speak,
No blame belongs to thee :) Ventidius lately
Buried his Father, by whose death he's stepp'd
Into a great estate : When he was poor,
Imprison'd, and in scarcity of friends,
I clear'd him with five Talents : Greet him from me,
Bid him suppose, some good necessity
Touches his Friend, which craves to be remember'd
With those five Talents; that had, giv't these fellows
To whom 'tis instant due. Nev'r speak, or think,
That Timon's fortunes 'mong his friends can sink.

STEWARD: I would I could not think it :
That thought is Bounty's foe;
Being free itself, it thinks all others so.

                    Exeunt.

III. 1

Flaminius waiting to speak with a Lord from his Master,
enters a servant to him.

SERVANT: I have told my Lord of you, he is coming down
to you.

FLAMINIUS: I thank you Sir.

Enter Lucullus.

SERVANT: Here's my Lord.

LUCULLUS: One of Lord Timon's men? A gift I warrant.
Why this hits right: I dreamt of a silver bason and ewer
tonight. Flaminius, honest Flaminius, you are very respectively welcome sir. Fill me some wine. And how
does that Honourable, Complete, Free-hearted Gentleman of Athens thy very bountiful good Lord and
Master?

FLAMINIUS: His health is well sir.

LUCULLUS: I am right glad that his health is well sir:
and what hast thou there under thy Cloak, pretty Flaminius?

FLAMINIUS: Faith, nothing but an empty box Sir, which
in my Lord's behalf, I come to intreat your Honour to
supply: who having great and instant occasion to use
fifty Talents, hath sent to your Lordship to furnish him:
nothing doubting your present assistance therein.

LUCULLUS: La, la, la, la: Nothing doubting says he? Alas
good Lord, a noble Gentleman 'tis, if he would not keep
so good a house. Many a time and often I ha' din'd with
him, and told him on't, and come again to supper to him
of purpose, to have him spend less, and yet he would embrace no counsel, take no warning by my coming, every

man has his fault, and honesty is his. I ha' told him on't, but I could ne'er get him from't.

Enter Servant with Wine.

SERVANT: Please your Lordship, here is the wine.

LUCULLUS: Flaminius, I have noted thee always wise. Here's to thee.

FLAMINIUS: Your Lordship speaks your pleasure.

LUCULLUS: I have observed thee always for a towardly • prompt spirit, give thee thy due, and one that knows what belongs to reason; and canst use the time well, if the time use thee well. Good parts in thee; get you gone sirrah. Draw nearer honest Flaminius. Thy Lord's a bountiful Gentleman, but thou art wise, and thou know'st well enough (although thou com'st to me) that this is no time to lend money, especially upon bare friendship without security. Here's three solidares for thee, good Boy wink at me, and say thou saw'st me not. Fare thee well.

FLAMINIUS: Is't possible the world should so much differ, And we alive that lived? Fly damned baseness To him that worships thee.

LUCULLUS: Ha? Now I see thou art a Fool, and fit for thy Master.

Exit Lucullus.

FLAMINIUS: May these add to the number that may scald thee:

Let molten coin be thy damnation,

Thou disease of a friend, and not himself:

Has friendship such a faint and milky heart,

It turns in less than two nights? O you Gods!

I feel my Master's passion. This slave unto his honour,

Has my Lord's meat in him:

Why should it thrive, and turn to nutriment,

When he is turn'd to poison?
O may diseases only work upon't:
And when he's sick to death, let not that part of Nature
Which my Lord paid for, be of any power
To expell sickness, but prolong his hour.

Exit.

III. 2

Enter Lucius, with three strangers.

LUCIUS: Who the Lord Timon? He is my very good friend and an honourable Gentleman.

1 STRANGER: We know him for no less, though we are but strangers to him. But I can tell you one thing my Lord, and which I hear from common rumours, now Lord Timon's happy hours are done and past, and his estate shrinks from him.

LUCIUS: Fie no, do not believe it: he cannot want for money.

2 STRANGER: But believe you this my Lord, that not long ago, one of his men was with the Lord Lucullus, to borrow so many Talents, nay urg'd extremely for't, and showed what necessity belong'd to't, and yet was denied.

LUCIUS: How?

2 STRANGER: I tell you, denied my Lord.

LUCIUS: What a strange case was that? Now before the Gods I am ashamed on't. Denied that honorable man? There was very little honour show'd in't. For my own part, I must needs confess, I have received some small kindnesses from him, as money, plate, jewels, and such like trifles; nothing comparing to his: yet had he mistook him, and sent to me, I should ne'er have denied his occasion so many Talents.

Enter Servilius.

SERVILIUS: See, by good hap yonder's my Lord, I have sweat to see his Honour. My Honour'd Lord.

LUCIUS: Servilius? You are kindly met sir. Fare thee well, commend me to thy honourable virtuous Lord, my very exquisite Friend.

SERVILIUS: May it please your Honour, my Lord hath sent –

LUCIUS: Ha? what has he sent? I am so much endeared to that Lord; he's ever sending: how shall I thank him think'st thou? And what has he sent now?

SERVILIUS: Has only sent his present occasion now my Lord: requesting your Lordship to supply his instant use with so many Talents.

LUCIUS: I know his Lordship is but merry with me,
He cannot want fifty five hundred Talents.

SERVILIUS: But in the meantime he wants less my Lord.
If his occasion were not virtuous,
I should not urge it half so faithfully.

LUCIUS: Dost thou speak seriously Servilius?

SERVILIUS: Upon my soul 'tis true Sir.

LUCIUS: What a wicked beast was I to disfurnish myself against such a good time, when I might ha' shown myself honourable? How unluckily it happen'd, that I should purchase the day before for a little part, and undo a great deal of honour? Servilius, now before the Gods I am not able to do (the more beast I say) I was sending to use Lord Timon myself, these Gentlemen can witness; but I would not for the wealth of Athens I had done't now. Commend me bountifully to his good Lordship, and I hope his Honour will conceive the fairest of me, because I have no power to be kind. And tell him this from me, I count it one of my greatest afflictions say, that

I cannot pleasure such an Honourable Gentleman. Good
Servilius, will you befriend me so far, as to use mine own
words to him?

SERVILIUS: Yes sir, I shall.

Exit Servilius.

LUCIUS: I'll look you out a good turn, Servilius.
True as you said, Timon is shrunk indeed,
And he that's once denied, will hardly speed.

Exit.

1 STRANGER: Do you observe this Hostilius?

2 STRANGER: Ay, too well.
Why this is the world's soul,
And just of the same piece
Is every Flatterer's sport: who can call him his friend
That dips in the same dish? For in my knowing
Timon has been this Lord's Father,
And kept his credit with his purse:
Supported his estate, nay Timon's money
Has paid his men their wages. He ne'er drinks,
But Timon's silver treads upon his lip,
And yet, oh see the monstrousness of man,
When he looks out in an ungrateful shape;
He does deny him (in respect of his)
What charitable men afford to beggars.

3 STRANGER: Religion groans at it.

1 STRANGER: For mine own part, I never tasted Timon in
my life
Nor came any of his bounties over me,
To mark me for his Friend. Yet I protest,
For his right noble mind, illustrious virtue,
And honourable carriage,
Had his necessity made use of me,
I would have put my wealth into donation,

And the best half should have return'd to him,
So much I love his heart: But I perceive,
Men must learn now with pity to dispense,
For Policy sits above Conscience.

Exeunt.

III. 3

Enter a third servant with Sempronius, another o,
Timon's Friends.

SEMPRONIUS: Must he needs trouble me in't? Hum..
   'Bove all others?
   He might have tried Lord Lucius, or Lucullus,
   And now Ventidius is wealthy too,
   Whom he redeem'd from prison. All these
   Owes their estates unto him.
SERVANT: My Lord,
   They have all been touch'd, and found base metal,
   For they have all denied him.
SEMPRONIUS: How? Have they denied him?
   Has Ventidius and Lucullus denied him,
   And does he send to me? Three? Humh!
   It shows but little love, or judgement in him.
   Must I be his last refuge? His Friends (like Physicians)
   Thrive, give him over: Must I take th'cure upon me?
   Has much disgrac'd me in't, I'm angry at him,
   That might have known my place. I see no sense for't,
   But his occasions might have wooed me first:
   For in my conscience, I was the first man
   That ere received gift from him.
   And does he think so backwardly of me now,
   That I'll requite it last? No:
   So it may prove an argument of laughter

To th'rest, and 'mong'st Lords be thought a Fool:
I'd rather than the worth of thrice the sum,
Had sent to me first, but for my mind's sake:
I'd such a courage to do him good. But now return,
And with their faint reply, this answer join;
Who bates mine honour, shall not know my coin.

Exit.

SERVANT: Excellent: Your Lordship's a goodly villain:
the devil knew not what he did, when he made man
politic; he crossed himself by't: and I cannot think, but
in the end, the villainies of man will set him clear. How
fairly this Lord strives to appear foul? Takes virtuous
copies to be wicked: like those, that under hot ardent
zeal, would set whole Realms on fire, of such a nature is
his politic love.

This was my Lord's best hope, now all are fled
Save only the Gods. Now his Friends are dead.
Doors that were ne're acquainted with their wards
Many a bounteous year, must be employ'd
Now to guard sure their Master:
And this is all a liberal course allows,
Who cannot keep his wealth, must keep his house.

Exit.

III.4

*Enter Varro's man, meeting others. All Timon's
Creditors to wait for his coming out. Then enter
Lucius and Hortensius.*

VARRO'S MAN: Well met, good morrow Titus and Hortensius.

TITUS: The like to you kind Varro.

HORTENSIUS: Lucius, what do we meet together:

LUCIUS: Ay, and I think one business does command us all.
  For mine is money.
TITUS: So is theirs, and ours.

Enter Philotus.

LUCIUS: And sir Philotus too.
PHILOTUS: Good day at once.
LUCIUS: Welcome good Brother.
  What do you think the hour?
PHILOTUS: Labouring for nine.
LUCIUS: So much?
PHILOTUS: Is not my Lord seen yet?
LUCIUS: Not yet.
PHILOTUS: I wonder on't, he was wont to shine at seven.
LUCIUS: Ay, but the days are waxed shorter with him:
  You must consider, that a prodigal course
  Is like the Sun's, but not like his recoverable, I fear:
  'Tis deepest winter in Lord Timon's purse, that is: One
  may reach deep enough, and yet find little.
PHILOTUS: I am of your ear, for that.
TITUS: I'll show you how t'observe a strange event:
  Your Lord sends now for money?
HORTENSIUS: Most true, he does.
TITUS: And he wears jewels now of Timon's gift,
  For which I wait for money.
HORTENSIUS: It is against my heart.
LUCIUS: Mark how strange it shows,
  Timon in this, should pay more than he owes:
  And e'en as if your Lord should wear rich jewels,
  And send for money for'em.
HORTENSIUS: I'm weary of this charge,
  The Gods can witness:
  I know my Lord hath spent of Timon's wealth,
  And now ingratitude, makes it worse than stealth.

VARRO: Yes, mine's three thousand Crowns:
   What's yours?

LUCIUS: Five thousand mine.

VARRO: 'Tis much deep, and it should seem by th'sum
   Your Master's confidence was above mine,
   Else surely his had equal'd.

Enter Flaminius.

TITUS: One of Lord Timon's men.

LUCIUS: Flaminius? Sir, a word: Pray is my Lord ready to
   come forth?

FLAMINIUS: No, indeed he is not.

TITUS: We attend his Lordship: pray signify so much.

FLAMINIUS: I need not tell him that, he knows you are too
   diligent.

Enter Steward in a cloak, muffled.

LUCIUS: Ha: is not that his Steward muffled so?
   He goes away in a cloud: Call him, call him.

TITUS: Do you hear, sir?

2 VARRO'S MAN: By your leave, sir.

STEWARD: What do ye ask of me, my Friend.

TITUS: We wait for certain money here, sir.

STEWARD: Ay, if money were as certain as your waiting.
   'Twere sure enough.
   Why then preferr'd you not your sums and bills
   When your false Masters eat of my Lord's meat?
   Then they could smile, and fawn upon his debts,
   And take down th'interest into their glutt'nous maws.
   You do yourselves but wrong, to stir me up,
   Let me pass quietly:
   Believe't, my Lord and I have made an end,
   I have no more to reckon, he to spend.

LUCIUS: Ay, but this answer will not serve.

STEWARD: If't'twill not serve, 'tis not so base as you,

For you serve Knaves.

1 VARRO'S MAN: How? What does his cashier'd Worship mutter?

2 VARRO'S MAN: No matter what, he's poor, and that's revenge enough. Who can speak broader, than he that has no house to put his head in? Such may rail against great buildings.

Enter Servilius.

TITUS: Oh here's Servilius: now we shall know some answer.

SERVILIUS: If I might beseech you Gentlemen, to repair some other hour, I should derive much from't. For take't of my soul, my Lord leans wondrously to discontent: His comfortable temper has forsook him, he's much out of health, and keeps his chamber.

LUCIUS: Many do keep their chambers, are not sick:
And if it be so far beyond his health,
Methinks he should the sooner pay his debts,
And make a clear way to the Gods.

SERVILIUS: Good Gods.

TITUS: We cannot take this for answer, sir.

FLAMINIUS: *Within.* Servilius help, my Lord, my Lord.

Enter Timon in a rage.

TIMON: What, are my doors oppos'd against my passage?
Have I been ever free, and must my house
Be my retentive enemy? My jail?
The place which I have feasted, does it now
(Like all Mankind) show me an iron heart?

LUCIUS: Put in now Titus.

TITUS: My Lord, here is my bill.

LUCIUS: Here's mine.

1 VARRO'S MAN: And mine, my Lord.

2 VARRO'S MAN: And ours, my Lord.

PHILOTUS: All our bills.

TIMON: Knock me down with 'em, cleave me to the girdle.

LUCIUS: Alas, my Lord.

TIMON: Cut my heart in sums.

TITUS: Mine, fifty talents.

TIMON: Tell out my blood.

LUCIUS: Five thousand crowns, my Lord.

TIMON: Five thousand drops pays that.
What yours? and yours?

1 VARRO'S MAN: My Lord.

2 VARRO'S MAN: My Lord.

TIMON: Tear me, take me, and the Gods fall upon you.

Exit Timon.

HORTENSIUS: Faith I perceive our Masters may throw their caps at their money, these debts may well be call'd desperate ones, for a madman owes 'em.

Exeunt.

Enter Timon.

TIMON: They have e'en put my breath from me the slaves. Creditors? Devils.

STEWARD: My dear Lord.

TIMON: What if it should be so?

STEWARD: My Lord.

TIMON: I'll have it so. My Steward?

STEWARD: Here my Lord.

TIMON: So fitly? Go, bid all my Friends again, Lucius, Lucullus, and Sempronius Ullorxa: All, I'll once more feast the rascals.

STEWARD: O my Lord, you only speak from you distracted soul; there's not so much left to furnish out a moderate table.

TIMON: Be it not in thy care:

Go I charge thee, invite them all, let in the tide
Of Knaves once more: my Cook and I'll provide.
Exeunt.

III. 5

*Enter three Senators at one door, Alcibiades meeting
them, with Attendants.*

1 SENATOR: My Lord, you have my voice, to't.
The fault's bloody:
'Tis necessary he should die:
Nothing emboldens sin so much, as mercy.

2 SENATOR: Most true; the Law shall bruise 'em.

ALCIBIADES: Honour, health, and compassion to the
Senate.

1 SENATOR: Now Captain.

ALCIBIADES: I am an humble suitor to your virtues;
For pity is the virtue of the Law,
And none but Tyrants use it cruelly.
It pleases time and Fortune to lie heavy
Upon a Friend of mine, who in hot blood
Hath stepp'd into the Law: which is past depth
To those that (without heed) do plunge into't.
He is a man (setting his fate aside) of comely virtues,
Nor did he soil the fact with cowardice,
(And honour in him, which buys out his fault)
But with a noble fury, and fair spirit,
Seeing his reputation touch'd to death,
He did oppose his foe:
And with such sober and unnoted passion
He did behoove his anger ere 'twas spent,
As if he had but prov'd an argument.

1 SENATOR: You undergo too strict a paradox,

c

Striving to make an ugly deed look fair:
Your words have took such pains, as if they labour'd
To bring manslaughter into form, and set quarreling
Upon the head of valour; which indeed
Is valour mis-begot, and came into the world,
When Sects, and Factions were newly born.
He's truly valiant, that can wisely suffer
The worst that man can breathe,
And make his wrongs, his outsides,
To wear them like his raiment, carelessly,
And ne'er prefer his injuries to his heart,
To bring it into danger.
If wrongs be evils, and enforce us kill,
What folly 'tis, to hazard life for ill.

ALCIBIADES: My Lord.

1 SENATOR: You cannot make gross sins look clear,
To revenge is no valour, but to bear.

ALCIBIADES: My Lords, then under favour, pardon me,
If I speak like a Captain.
Why do fond men expose themselves to battle,
And not endure all threats? Sleep upon't,
And let the foes quietly cut their throats
Without repugnancy? If there be
Such valour in the bearing, what make we
Abroad? Why then, women are more valiant
That stay at home, if bearing carry it:
And the Ass, more Captain than the Lion?
The fellow loaden with irons, wiser than the Judge?
If wisdom be in suffering, oh my Lords,
As you are great, be pitifully good,
Who cannot condemn rashness in cold blood?
To kill, I grant, is sin's extremest gust,
But in defence, by mercy, 'tis most just.

To be in anger, is impiety:
But who is man, that is not angry.
Weigh but the crime with this.

2 SENATOR: You breathe in vain.

ALCIBIADES: In vain?
His service done at Lacedemon, and Bizantium,
Were a sufficient briber for his life.

1 SENATOR: What's that?

ALCIBIADES: Why say my Lords ha's done fair service,
And slain in fight many of your enemies:
How full of valour did he bear himself
In the last conflict, and made plenteous wounds?

2 SENATOR: He has made too much plenty with him:
He's a sworn rioter, he has a sin
That often drowns him, and takes his valour prisoner.
If there were no foes, that were enough
To overcome him. In that beastly fury,
He has been known to commit outrages,
And cherish factions. 'Tis inferr'd to us,
His days are foul, and his drink dangerous.

1 SENATOR: He dies.

ALCIBIADES: Hard fate: he might have died in war.
My Lords, if not for any parts in him,
Though his right arm might purchase his own time,
And be in debt to none: yet more to move you,
Take my deserts to his, and join 'em both.
And for I know, your reverend ages love security,
I'll pawn my victories, all my honour to you
Upon his good returns.
If by this crime, he owes the Law his life,
Why let the war receive't in valiant gore,
For Law is strict, and war is nothing more.

1 SENATOR: We are for Law, he dies, urge it no more

On height of our displeasure: Friend, or brother,
He forfeits his own blood, that spills another.

ALCIBIADES: Must it be so? It must not be:
My Lords, I do beseech you know me.

2 SENATOR: How?

ALCIBIADES: Call me to your remembrances.

3 SENATOR: What.

ALCIBIADES: I cannot think but your age has forgot me,
It could not else be, I should prove so base,
To sue and be denied such common grace.
My wounds ache at you.

1 SENATOR: Do you dare our anger?
'Tis in few words, but spacious in effect:
We banish thee forever.

ALCIBIADES: Banish me?
Banish your dotage, banish usury.
That makes the Senate ugly.

1 SENATOR: If after two days shine, Athens contain thee,
Attend our weightier judgement.
And not to swell our spirit,
He shall be executed presently.
                                        Exeunt.

ALCIBIADES: Now the Gods keep you old enough,
That you may live
Only in bone, that none may look on you.
I'm worse than mad: I have kept back their foes
While they have told their money, and let out
Their coin upon large interest. I myself,
Rich only in large hurts. All those, for this?
Is this the balsam, that the usuring Senate
Powers into Captains' wounds? Banishment.
It comes not ill: I hate not to be banish'd,
It is a cause worthy my spleen and fury,

Act Three, Scene Five   69

That I may strike at Athens. I'll cheer up
My discontented troops, and lay for hearts;
'Tis honour with most lands to be at odds,
Soldiers should brook as little wrongs as Gods.

Exit.

III.6

Enter divers Friends at several doors.

1 FRIEND: The good time of day to you, sir.

2 FRIEND: I also wish it to you: I think this Honourable
Lord did but try us this other day.

1 FRIEND: Upon that were my thoughts tiring when we
encounter'd. I hope it is not so low with him as he made
it seem in the trial of his several Friends.

2 FRIEND: It should not be, by the persuasion of his new
feasting.

1 FRIEND: I should think so. He hath sent me an earnest
inviting, which many my near occasions did urge me to
put off: but he hath conjur'd me beyond them, and I
must needs appear.

2 FRIEND: In like manner was I in debt to my importunate
business, but he would not hear my excuse. I am sorry,
when he sent to borrow of me, that my provision was
out.

1 FRIEND: I am sick of that grief too, as I understand how
all things go.

2 FRIEND: Every man hears so: what would he have borrowed of you?

1 FRIEND: A thousand pieces.

2 FRIEND: A thousand pieces?

1 FRIEND: What of you?

2 FRIEND: He sent to me sir – Here he comes.

Enter Timon and Attendants.

TIMON: With all my heart Gentlemen both; and how fare you?

1 FRIEND: Ever at the best, hearing well of your Lordship.

2 FRIEND: The swallow follows not summer more willing, than we your Lordship.

TIMON: Nor more willingly leaves winter, such summer birds are men. Gentlemen, our dinner will not recompence this long stay: Feast your ears with the music awhile: If they will fare so harshly o'th'trumpets sound: we shall to't presently.

1 FRIEND: I hope it remains not unkindly with your Lordship, that I return'd you an empty Messenger.

TIMON: O sir, let it not trouble you.

2 FRIEND: My Noble Lord.

TIMON: Ah my good Friend, what cheer?

The Banquet brought in.

2 FRIEND: My most Honourable Lord, I am e'en sick of shame, that when your Lordship this other day sent to me, I was so unfortunate a beggar.

TIMON: Think not on't, sir.

2 FRIEND: If you had sent but two hours before.

TIMON: Let it not cumber your better remembrance. Come bring in all together.

2 FRIEND: All cover'd dishes.

1 FRIEND: Royal cheer, I warrant you.

3 FRIEND: Doubt not that, if money and the season can yield it.

1 FRIEND: How do you? What's the news?

3 FRIEND: Alcibiades is banish'd: hear you of it?

BOTH: Alcibiades banish'd?

3 FRIEND: 'Tis so, be sure of it.

1 FRIEND: How? How?

2 FRIEND: I pray you upon what?

TIMON: My worthy Friends, will you draw near?

3 FRIEND: I'll tell you more anon. Here's a noble feast toward.

2 FRIEND: This is the old man still.

3 FRIEND: Wilt hold? Wilt hold?

2 FRIEND: It does: but time will, and so.

3 FRIEND: I do conceive.

TIMON: Each man to his stool, with that spur as he would to the lip of his Mistress: your diet shall be in all places alike. Make not a City Feast of it, to let the meat cool, ere we can agree upon the first place. Sit, sit. The Gods require our thanks.

You great Benefactors, sprinkle our society with thankfulness. For your own gifts, make yourselves prais'd: But reserve still to give, lest your Deities be despised. Lend to each man enough, that one needs not lend to another. For were your Godheads to borrow of men, men would forsake the Gods. Make the meat be beloved, more than the man that gives it. Let no Assembly of twenty, be without a score of villains. If there sit twelve women at the Table, let a dozen of them be as they are. The rest of your fees, O Gods, the Senators of Athens, together with the common leg of People, what is amiss in them, you Gods, make suitable for destruction. For these my present Friends, as they are to me nothing, so in nothing bless them, and to nothing are they welcome.

Uncover Dogs, and lap.

Some speak: What does his Lordship mean?

Some other: I know not.

TIMON: May you a better Feast never behold
You knot of Mouth-Friends: Smoke, and lukewarm water
Is your perfection. This is Timon's last,

Who stuck and spangled you with flatteries,
Washes it off and sprinkles in your faces
Your reeking villainy. Live loath'd, and long
Most smiling, smooth, detested parasites,
Courteous destroyers, affable wolves, meek bears:
You Fools of Fortune, trencher-friends, Time's flies,
Cap and knee slaves, vapours, and minute jacks.
Of man and beast, the infinite malady
Crust you quite o'er. What dost thou go?
Soft, take thy physic first; thou too, and thou:
Stay I will lend thee money, borrow none.
What? All in motion? Henceforth be no Feast,
Whereat a villain's not a welcome guest.
Burn house, sink Athens, henceforth hated be
Of Timon Man, and all Humanity.

Exit.

Enter the Senators, with other Lords.

1 SENATOR: How now, my Lords?

2 SENATOR: Know you the quality of Lord Timon's fury?

3 SENATOR: Push, did you see my cap?

4 SENATOR: I have lost my gown.

1 SENATOR: He's but a mad Lord, and nought but humours sways him. He gave me a jewel th'other day, and now he has beat it out of my hat.
Did you see my jewel?

2 SENATOR: Did you see my cap.

3 SENATOR: Here'tis.

4 SENATOR: Here lies my gown.

1 SENATOR: Let's make no stay.

2 SENATOR: Lord Timon's mad.

3 SENATOR: I feel't upon my bones.

4 SENATOR: One day he gives us diamonds, next day stones.   *Exeunt the Senators.*

Enter Timon.

TIMON: Let me look back upon thee. O thou Wall
That girdles in those wolves, dive in the earth,
And fence not Athens. Matrons, turn incontinent,
Obedience fail in children: slaves and fools
Pluck the grave wrinkled Senate from the Bench,
And minister in their steads, to general filths.
Convert o'th'instant green Virginity,
Do't in your parents' eyes. Bankrupts, hold fast
Rather than render back; out with your knives,
And cut your trusters' throats. Bound servants, steal,
Large-handed robbers your grave Masters are,
And pill by Law. Maid, to thy Master's bed,
Thy Mistress is o'th'brothell. Son of sixteen,
Pluck the lin'd crutch from thy old limping Sire,
With it, beat out his brains. Piety, and fear,
Religion to the Gods, Peace, Justice, Truth,
Domestick awe, Night-rest, and Neighborhood,
Instruction, Manners, Mysteries, and Trades,
Degrees, Observances, Customs, and Laws,
Decline to your confounding contraries.
And yet Confusion live: Plagues incident to men,
Your potent and infectious Fevers, heap
On Athens ripe for stroke. Thou cold Sciatica,
Cripple our Senators, that their limbs may halt
As lamely as their manners. Lust, and Liberty
Creep in the minds and marrows of our youth,
That 'gainst the stream of Virtue they may strive,
And drown themselves in riot. Itches, Blains,

Sow all th'Athenian bosoms, and their crop
Be general leprosy: Breath infect breath,
That their society (as their friendship) may
Be merely poison. Nothing I'll bear from thee
But nakedness, thou detestable Town,
Take thou that too, with multiplying bans:
Timon will to the Woods, where he shall find
Th'unkindest beast, more kinder than Mankind.
The Gods confound (hear me you good Gods all)
Th'Athenians both within, and out that Wall:
And grant as Timon grows, his hate may grow
To the whole race of Mankind, high and low.
Amen.

Exit.

IV.2

Enter Steward with two or three Servants.

1 SERVANT: Hear you M. Steward, where's our Master?
 Are we undone, cast off, nothing remaining?

STEWARD: Alack my fellows, what should I say to you?
 Let me be recorded by the righteous Gods,
 I am as poor as you.

1 SERVANT: Such a House broke?
 So noble a Master fall'n, all gone, and not
 One Friend to take his Fortune by the arm,
 And go along with him.

2 SERVANT: As we do turn our backs
 From our companion, thrown into his grave,
 So his familiars to his buried fortunes
 Slink all away, leave their false vows with him
 Like empty purses pick'd; and his poor self
 A dedicated beggar to the air,

With his disease, of all shunn'd poverty,
Walks like contempt alone. More of our fellows.
Enter other Servants.

STEWARD: All broken implements of a ruin'd house.

3 SERVANT: Yet do our hearts wear Timon's livery,
That see I by our faces: we are Fellows still,
Serving alike in sorrow: Leak'd is our bark,
And we poor mates, stand on the dying deck,
Hearing the surges threat: we must all part
Into this sea of air.

STEWARD: Good fellows all,
The latest of my wealth I'll share among'st you.
Wherever we shall meet, for Timon's sake,
Let's yet be fellows. Let's shake our heads, and say
As 'twere a knell unto our Master's fortunes,
We have seen better days. Let each take some:
Nay put out all your hands: Not one word more,
Thus part we rich in sorrow, parting poor.
Embrace and part several ways.

Oh the fierce wretchedness that Glory brings us!
Who would not wish to be from wealth exempt,
Since Riches point to Misery and Contempt?
Who would be so mock'd with Glory, or to live
But in a dream of Friendship,
To have his pomp, and all what state compounds,
But only painted like his varnish'd friends:
Poor honest Lord, brought low by his own heart,
Undone by Goodness: Strange unusual blood,
When man's worst sin is, He does too much good.
Who then dares to be half so kind again?
For Bounty that makes Gods, do still mar men.
My dearest Lord, bless'd to be most accurs'd,
Rich only to be wretched; thy great fortunes

Are made thy chief afflictions. Alas (kind Lord)
He's flung in rage from this ungrateful seat
Of monstrous Friends:
Nor has he with him to supply his life,
Or that which can command it:
I'll follow and inquire him out.
I'll ever serve his mind, with my best will,
Whilst I have gold, I'll be his Steward still.

Exit.

IV.3

Enter Timon in the woods.

TIMON: O blessed breeding Sun, draw from the earth
Rotten humidity: below thy Sister's Orb
Infect the air. Twinn'd Brothers of one womb,
Whose procreation, residence, and birth,
Scarce is dividant; touch them with several fortunes,
The greater scorns the lesser. Not Nature
(To whom all sores lay siege) can bear great fortune
But by contempt of Nature.
Raise me this Beggar, and deny't that Lord,
The Senators shall bear contempt hereditary,
The Beggar native honour.
It is the Pastor lards, the brother's sides,
The want that makes him leave: who dares? who dares
In purity of manhood stand upright
And say, this man's a Flatterer. If one be,
So are they all: for every grize of Fortune
Is smooth'd by that below. The learned pate
Ducks to the Golden Fool. All's obliquy:
There's nothing level in our cursed natures
But direct villainy. Therefore be abhorr'd,

All feasts, societies, and throngs of men.
His semblable, yea himself Timon disdains,
Destruction fang mankind; Earth yield me roots,
Who seeks for better of thee, sauce his palate
With thy most operant poison. What is here?
Gold? Yellow, glittering, precious gold?
No Gods, I am no idle votarist,
Roots you clear Heavens. Thus much of this will make
Black, white; foul, fair; wrong, right;
Base, noble; old, young; coward, valiant.
Ha you Gods! why this? what this, you Gods? why this
Will lug your priests and servants from your sides:
Pluck stout men's pillows from below their heads.
This yellow Slave,
Will knit and break Religions, bless th'accurs'd,
Make the hoar leprosy ador'd, place thieves,
And give them title, knee, and approbation
With Senators on the Bench: This is it
That makes the wappen'd widow wed again;
She, whom the Spittle-house, and ulcerous sores,
Would cast the gorge at. This embalms and spices
To'th'April day again. Come damn'd Earth,
Thou common whore of Mankind, that puts odds
Among the rout of Nations, I will make thee
Do thy right nature.

March afar off.

Ha? A Drum? Th'art quick,
But yet I'll bury thee: Thou't go (strong Thief)
When gouty keepers of thee cannot stand:
Nay stay thou out for earnest.

 Enter Alcibiades with Drum and Fife in warlike
  manner, and Phrynia and Timandra.

ALCIBIADES: What art thou there? speak.

TIMON: A beast as thou art. The canker gnaw thy heart
For showing me again the eyes of man.

ALCIBIADES: What is thy name? Is man so hateful to thee,
That art thyself a man?

TIMON: I am Misantropos, and hate Mankind.
For thy part, I do wish thou wert a dog,
That I might love thee something.

ALCIBIADES: I know thee well:
But in thy fortunes am unlearn'd, and strange.

TIMON: I know thee too, and more than that I know thee
I not desire to know. Follow thy drum,
With man's blood, paint the ground gules, gules:
Religious canons, civil laws are cruel,
Then what should war be? This fell whore of thine,
Hath in her more destruction than thy sword,
For all her cherubin look.

PHRYNIA: Thy lips rot off.

TIMON: I will not kiss thee, then the rot returns
To thine own lips again.

ALCIBIADES: How came the noble Timon to this change?

TIMON: As the Moon does, by wanting light to give:
But then renew I could not like the Moon,
There were no Suns to borrow of.

ALCIBIADES: Noble Timon, what friendship may I do thee?

TIMON: None, but to maintain my opinion.

ALCIBIADES: What is it Timon?

TIMON: Promise me friendship, but perform none. If thou wilt not promise, the Gods plague thee, for thou art a man: if thou dost perform, confound thee, for thou art a man.

ALCIBIADES: I have heard in some sort of thy miseries.

TIMON: Thou saw'st them when I had prosperity.

ALCIBIADES: I see them now, then was a blessed time.

TIMON: As thine is now, held with a brace of harlots,

TIMANDRA: Is this th'Athenian minion, whom the world
   Voic'd so regardfully?

TIMON: Art thou Timandra?

TIMANDRA: Yes.

TIMON: Be a whore still, they love thee not that use thee,
   give them diseases, leaving with thee their lust. Make use
   of thy salt hours, season the slaves for tubs and baths,
   bring down rose-cheek'd youth to the fubfast, and the
   diet.

TIMANDRA: Hang thee Monster.

ALCIBIADES: Pardon him sweet Timandra, for his wits
   Are drown'd and lost in his calamities.
   I have but little gold of late, brave Timon,
   The want whereof, doth daily make revolt
   In my penurious Band. I have heard and griev'd
   How cursed Athens, mindless of thy worth,
   Forgetting thy great deeds, when neighbour states
   But for thy sword and fortune trod upon them.

TIMON: I prithee beat thy Drum, and get thee gone.

ALCIBIADES: I am thy Friend, and pity thee dear Timon.

TIMON: How dost thou pity him whom thou dost trouble,
   I had rather be alone.

ALCIBIADES: Why fare thee well:
   Here is some gold for thee.

TIMON: Keep it, I cannot eat it.

ALCIBIADES: When I have laid proud Athens on a heap.

TIMON. War'st thou 'gainst Athens?

ALCIBIADES: Ay Timon, and have cause.

TIMON: The Gods confound them all in thy conquest.

And thee after, when thou hast conquer'd.

ALCIBIADES: Why me, Timon?

TIMON: That by killing of villains
Thou was't born to conquer my Country.
Put up thy gold. Go on, here's gold, go on;
Be as a planetary plague, when Jove
Will o'er some high-vic'd City, hang his poison
In the sick air: let not thy sword skip one:
Pity not honour'd Age for his white beard,
He is an usurer. Strike me the counterfeit matron
It is her habit only, that is honest,
Herself's a bawd. Let not the virgin's cheek
Make soft thy trenchant sword: for those milk paps
That through the window barn bore at men's eyes,
Are not within the leaf of pity writ,
But set them down horrible traitors. Spare not the babe
Whose dimpled smiles from fools exhaust their mercy;
Think it a bastard, whom the Oracle
Hath doubtfully pronounced, the throat shall cut,
And mince it sans remorse. Swear against objects,
Put armour on thine ears, and on thine eyes,
Whose proof, nor yells of mothers, maids, nor babes,
Nor sight of Priests in holy vestments bleeding,
Shall pierce a jot. There's gold to pay thy soldiers,
Make large confusion: and thy fury spent,
Confounded be thyself. Speak not, be gone.

ALCIBIADES: Hast thou gold yet, I'll take the gold thou
givest me, not all thy counsel.

TIMON: Dost thou or dost thou not, Heaven's curse upon
thee.

BOTH WHORES: Give us some gold good Timon, hast
thou more?

TIMON: Enough to make a whore forswear her trade,

And to make whores, a bawd. Hold up you sluts
Your aprons mountant; you are not othable,
Although I know you'll swear, terribly swear
Into strong shudders, and to heavenly agues
Th'immortal Gods that hear you. Spare your oaths:
I'll trust to your conditions, be whores still,
And he whose pious breath seeks to convert you,
Be strong in whore, allure him, burn him up,
Let your close fire predominate his smoke,
And be no turn-coats: yet may your pains six months
Be quite contrary. And thatch
Your poor thin roofs with burthens of the dead,
(Some that were hang'd) no matter:
Wear them, betray with them; Whore still,
Paint till a horse may mire upon your face:
A pox of wrinkles.
BOTH WHORES: Well, more gold, what then?
Believ't that we'll do anything for gold.
TIMON: Consumptions sow
In hollow bones of man, strike their sharp shins,
And mar men's spurring. Crack the Lawyer's voice,
That he may never more false title plead,
Nor sound his quillets shrilly: Hoar the Flamen,
That scold'st against the quality of flesh,
And not believes himself. Down with the nose,
Down with it flat, take the bridge quite away
Of him, that his particular to foresee
Smells from the general weal. Make curl'd pate ruffians
    bald
And let the unscarr'd braggarts of the War
Derive some pain from you. Plague all,
That your activity may defeat and quell
The source of all erection. There's more gold.

Do you damn others, and let this damn you.
And ditches grave you all.

BOTH WHORES: More counsel with more money, bounteous Timon.

TIMON: More whore, more mischief first, I have given you
earnest.

ALCIBIADES: Strike up the Drum towards Athens, farewell Timon: if I thrive well, I'll visit thee again.

TIMON: If I hope well, I'll never see thee more.

ALCIBIADES: I never did thee harm.

TIMON: Yes, thou spok'st well of me.

ALCIBIADES: Call'st thou that harm?

TIMON: Men daily find it. Get thee away,
And take thy beagles with thee.

ALCIBIADES: We but offend him, strike.

Exeunt.

TIMON: That Nature being sick of man's unkindness
Should yet be hungry: Common Mother, thou
Whose womb unmeasurable, and infinite breast
Teems and feeds all: whose selfsame mettle
Whereof thy proud child (arrogant man) is puff'd,
Engenders the black toad, and adder blue,
The gilded newt, and eyeless venom'd worm,
With all th'abhorred births below crisp Heaven,
Whereon Hyperion's quick'ning fire doth shine:
Yield him, who all the human sons do hate,
From forth thy plenteous bosom, one poor root:
Ensear thy fertile and conceptious womb,
Let it no more bring out ungrateful man.
Go great with tigers, dragons, wolves, and bears,
Teem with new monsters, whom thy upward face
Hath to the marbled mansion all above
Never presented. O, a root, dear thanks:

Dry up thy marrows, vines, and plough-torn leas,
Whereof ungrateful man with liquorish draughts
And morsels unctuous, greases his pure mind,
That from it all consideration slips –

Enter Apemantus.

More man? Plague, plague.

APEMANTUS: I was directed hither. Men report,
Thou dost affect my manners, and dost use them.

TIMON: Tis then, because thou dost not keep a dog
Whom I would imitate. Consumption catch thee.

APEMANTUS: This is in thee a nature but infected,
A poor unmanly melancholy sprung
From change of future. Why this spade? this place?
This slave-like habit, and these looks of care?
Thy flatterers yet wear silk, drink wine, lie soft,
Hug their diseas'd perfumes, and have forgot
That ever Timon was. Shame not these woods,
By putting on the cunning of a Carper.
Be thou a Flatterer now, and seek to thrive
By that which has undone thee; hinge thy knee,
And let his very breath whom thou'lt observe
Blow off thy cap: praise his most vicious strain,
And call it excellent: thou wast told thus:
Thou gav'st thine ears (like tapsters, that bad welcome)
To knaves, and all approachers: 'Tis most just
That thou turn rascal, had'st thou wealth again,
Rascals should have't. Do not assume my likeness.

TIMON: Were I like thee, I'd throw away myself.

APEMANTUS: Thou hast cast away thyself, being like thy-
self
A madman so long, now a fool: what think'st
That the bleak air, thy boisterous chamberlain
Will put thy shirt on warm? Will these moist trees,

That have out-liv'd the eagle, page thy heels
And skip when thou point'st out? Will the cold brook
Candied with ice, caudle thy morning taste
To cure thy o'er-night's surfeit? Call the creatures,
Whose naked natures live in all the spite
Of wreakful Heaven, whose bare unhoused trunks,
To the conflicting elements expos'd
Answer mere Nature: bid them flatter thee.
O thou shalt find.

TIMON: A fool of thee: depart.

APEMANTUS: I love thee better now, than ere I did.

TIMON: I hate thee worse.

APEMANTUS: Why?

TIMON: Thou flatter'st misery.

APEMANTUS: I flatter not, but say thou art a caitiff.

TIMON: Why do'st thou seek me out?

APEMANTUS: To vex thee.

TIMON: Always a villain's office, or a fool's.
  Dost please thyself in't?

APEMANTUS: Ay.

TIMON: What, a knave too?

APEMANTUS: If thou did'st put this sour cold habit on
  To castigate thy pride, 'twere well: but thou
  Dost it enforcedly: Thou'dst courtier be again
  Wert thou not beggar: willing misery
  Out-lives: incertain pomp, is crown'd before:
  The one is filling still, never complete:
  The other, at high wish: best state contentless,
  Hath a distracted and most wretched being,
  Worse than the worst, content.
  Thou should'st desire to die, being miserable.

TIMON: Not by his breath, that is more miserable.
  Thou art a slave, whom Fortune's tender arm

With favour never clasp'd: but bred a dog.
Had'st thou like us from our first swath proceeded,
The sweet degrees that this brief world affords,
To such as may the passive drugs of it
Freely command'st: thou would'st have plung'd thyself
In general riot, melted down thy youth
In different beds of lust, and never learn'd
The icy precepts of respect, but followed
The sugar'd game before thee. But myself,
Who had the world as my confectionary,
The mouths, the tongues, the eyes, and hearts of men,
At duty more than I could frame employment;
That numberless upon me stuck, as leaves
Do on the oak, have with one Winter's brush
Fell from their boughs, and left me open, bare,
For every storm that blows. I to bear this,
That never knew but better, is some burthen:
Thy nature, did commence in sufferance, Time
Hath made thee hard in't. Why should'st thou hate men?
They never flatter'd thee. What hast thou given?
If thou wilt curse; thy Father (that poor rag)
Must be thy subject; who in spite put stuff
To some she-beggar, and compounded thee
Poor rogue, hereditary. Hence, be gone,
If thou hadst not been born the worst of men,
Thou hadst been a knave and flatterer.

APEMANTUS: Art thou proud yet?

TIMON: Ay, that I am not thee.

APEMANTUS: Ay, that I was no prodigal.

TIMON: Ay, that I am one now.
  Were all the wealth I have shut up in thee,
  I'd give thee leave to hang it. Get thee gone:
  That the whole life of Athens were in this,

Thus would I eat it.

APEMANTUS: Here, I will mend thy feast.

TIMON: First mend thy company, take away thyself.

APEMANTUS: So I shall mend mine own, by th'lack of thine.

TIMON: 'Tis not well mended so, it is but botch'd;
If not, I would it were.

APEMANTUS: What would'st thou have to Athens?

TIMON: Thee thither in a whirlwind: if thou wilt,
Tell them there I have gold, look, so I have.

APEMANTUS: Here is no use for gold.

TIMON: The best, and truest:
For here it sleeps, and does no hired harm.

APEMANTUS: Where liest a nights Timon?

TIMON: Under that's above me.
Where feed'st thou a-days Apemantus?

APEMANTUS: Where my stomach finds meat, or rather where I eat it.

TIMON: Would poison were obedient, and knew my mind.

APEMANTUS: Where would'st thou send it?

TIMON: To sauce thy dishes.

APEMANTUS: The middle of Humanity thou never knewest, but the extremity of both ends. When thou wast in thy gilt, and thy perfume, they mock'd thee for too much curiosity: in thy rags thou know'st none, but art despis'd for the contrary. There's a medlar for thee, eat it.

TIMON: On what I hate, I feed not.

APEMANTUS: Dost hate a medlar?

TIMON: Ay, though it look like thee.

APEMANTUS: And th'hadst hated medlars sooner, thou should'st have loved thyself better now. What man did'st thou ever know unthrift, that was beloved after his means?

TIMON: Who without those means thou talk'st of, didst thou ever know belov'd?

APEMANTUS: Myself.

TIMON: I understand thee: thou had'st some means to keep a dog.

APEMANTUS: What things in the world canst thou nearest compare to thy flatterers?

TIMON: Women nearest, but men: men are the things themselves. What would'st thou do with the world Apemantus, if it lay in thy power?

APEMANTUS: Give it the beasts, to be rid of the men.

TIMON: Would'st thou have thyself fall in the confusion of men, and remain a beast with the beasts?

APEMANTUS: Ay Timon.

TIMON: A beastly ambition, which the Gods grant thee t'attain to. If thou wert the Lion, the Fox would beguile thee, if thou wert the Lamb, the Fox would eat thee: if thou wert the Fox, the Lion would suspect thee, when peradventure thou wert accus'd by the Ass: If thou wert the Ass, thy dullness would torment thee; and still thou liv'dst but as a breakfast to the Wolf. If thou were the Wolf, thy greediness would afflict thee, and oft thou should'st hazard thy life for thy dinner. Wert thou the Unicorn, pride and wrath would confound thee, and make thine own self the conquest of thy fury. Wert thou a Bear, thou would'st be kill'd by the Horse: wert thou a Horse, thou would'st be seiz'd by the Leopard: wert thou a Leopard, thou wert german to the Lion, and the spots of thy kindred, were jurors on thy life. All thy safety were remotion, and thy defence absence. What Beast could'st thou be, that were not subject to a Beast: and what a Beast thou art already, that seest not thy loss in transformation.

APEMANTUS: If thou could'st please me
    With speaking to me, thou might'st
    Have hit upon it here.
    The Commonwealth of Athens, is become
    A Forest of Beasts.

TIMON: How has the Ass broke the wall, that thou art out
    of the City.

APEMANTUS: Yonder comes a Poet and a Painter:
    The plague of company light upon thee:
    I will fear to catch it, and give way.
    When I know not what else to do,
    I'll see thee again.

TIMON: When there is nothing living but thee,
    Thou shalt be welcome.
    I had rather be a beggar's dog,
    Than Apemantus.

APEMANTUS: Thou art the cap
    Of all the Fools alive.

TIMON: Would thou wert clean enough
    To spit upon.

APEMANTUS: A plague on thee,
    Thou art too bad to curse.

TIMON: All villains
    That do stand by thee, are pure.

APEMANTUS: There is no leprosy,
    But what thou speak'st.

TIMON: If I name thee, I'll beat thee;
    But I should infect my hands.

APEMANTUS: I would my tongue
    Could rot them off.

TIMON: Away thou issue of a mangy dog.
    Choler does kill me,
    That thou art alive, I swoon to see thee.

APEMANTUS: Would thou would'st burst.

TIMON: Away thou tedious rogue, I am sorry I shall lose a stone by thee.

APEMANTUS: Beast.

TIMON: Slave.

APEMANTUS: Toad.

TIMON: Rogue, rogue, rogue.
  I am sick of this false world, and will love nought
  But even the mere necessities upon't:
  Then Timon presently prepare thy grave:
  Lie where the light foam of the sea may beat
  Thy gravestone daily, make thine Epitaph,
  That death in me, at others' lives may laugh.
  O thou sweet King-killer, and dear divorce
  Twixt natural Sun and fire: thou bright defiler
  Of Hymen's purest bed, thou valiant Mars,
  Thou ever, young, fresh, loved, and delicate wooer,
  Whose blush doth thaw the consecrated snow
  That lies on Dian's lap.
  Thou visible God,
  That souldrest close impossibilities,
  And mak'st them kiss; that speak'st with every tongue
  To every purpose: O thou touch of hearts,
  Think thy slave-man rebels, and by thy virtue
  Set them into confounding odds, that beasts
  May have the world in Empire.

APEMANTUS: Would 'twere so,
  But not till I am dead. I'll say th'hast gold:
  Thou wilt be throng'd too shortly.

TIMON: Throng'd too?

APEMANTUS: Ay.

TIMON: Thy back I prythee.

APEMANTUS: Live, and love thy misery.

TIMON: Long live so, and so die. I am quit.

APEMANTUS: Mo things like men,
Eat Timon, and abhor then.

Exit Apemantus.
Enter the Bandetti.

1 BANDETTO: Where should he have this gold? It is some
poor fragment, some slender ort of his remainder: the
mere want of gold, and the falling from of his Friends,
drove him into this melancholy.

2 BANDETTO: It is nois'd
He hath a mass of treasure.

3 BANDETTO: Let us make the assay upon him, if he care
not for't, he will supply us easily: if he covetously reserve
it, how shall's get it?

2 BANDETTO: True: for he bears it not about him:
'Tis hid.

1 BANDETTO: Is not this he?

ALL: Where?

2 BANDETTO: 'Tis his description.

3 BANDETTO: He? I know him.

ALL: Save thee Timon.

TIMON: Now thieves.

ALL: Soldiers, not thieves.

TIMON: Both too, and women's sons.

ALL: We are not thieves, but men
That much do want.

TIMON: Your greatest want is, you want much of meat:
Why should you want? Behold, the Earth hath roots:
Within this mile break forth a hundred springs:
The oaks bear mast, the briars scarlet heps,
The bounteous housewife Nature, on each bush,
Lays her full mess before you. Want? why want?

1 BANDETTO: We cannot live on grass, on berries, water,

As beasts, and birds, and fishes.

TIMON: Nor on the beasts themselves, the birds and fishes,
    You must eat men. Yet thanks I must you con,
    That you are thieves profess'd: that you work not
    In holier shapes: For there is boundless theft
    In limited professions. Rascal thieves
    Here's gold. Go, suck the subtle blood o'th'grape,
    Till the high fever seethe your blood to froth,
    And so scape hanging. Trust not the physician,
    His antidotes are poison, and he slays
    More than you rob: Take wealth, and lives together,
    Do villain do, since you protest to do't.
    Like workmen, I'll example you with thievery:
    The sun's a thief, and with his great attraction
    Robs the vast Sea. The Moon's an arrant thief,
    And her pale fire, she snatches from the Sun.
    The Sea's a thief, whose liquid surge, resolves
    The Moon into salt tears. The Earth's a thief,
    That feeds and breeds by a composture stolen
    From gen'ral excrement: each thing's a thief.
    The Laws, your curb and whip, in their rough power
    Has uncheck'd theft. Love not yourselves, away,
    Rob one another, there's more gold, cut throats,
    All that you meet are thieves: to Athens go,
    Break open shops, nothing can you steal
    But thieves do lose it: steal less, for this I give you,
    And gold confound you howsoe'er: Amen.

3 BANDETTO: Has almost charm'd me from my profession, by persuading me to it.

1 BANDETTO: 'Tis in the malice of mankind' that he thus advises us not to have us thrive in our mystery.

2 BANDETTO: I'll believe him as an enemy,
    And give over my trade.

1 BANDETTO: Let us first see peace in Athens, there is no time so miserable, but a man may be true.

Exit Thieves.
Enter the Steward to Timon.

STEWARD: Oh you Gods!
 Is yond despis'd and ruinous man my Lord?
 Full of decay and failing? Oh monument
 And wonder of good deeds, evilly bestow'd!
 What an alteration of honour has desp'rate want made?
 What viler thing upon the earth, than friends,
 Who can bring noblest minds, to basest ends.
 How rarely does it meet with this time's guise,
 When man was wish'd to love his enemies:
 Grant I may ever love, and rather woo
 Those that would mischief me, than those that do.
 Has caught me in his eye, I will present my honest grief
 unto him; and as my Lord, still serve him with my life.
 My dearest Master.

TIMON: Away: what art thou?

STEWARD: Have you forgot me, Sir?

TIMON: Why dost ask that? I have forgot all men.
 Then, if thou grunt'st, th'art a man.
 I have forgot thee.

STEWARD: An honest poor servant of yours.

TIMON: Then I know thee not:
 I never had honest man about me, ay all
 I kept were knaves, to serve in meat to villains.

STEWARD: The Gods are witness,
 Nev'r did poor Steward wear a truer grief
 For his undone Lord, than mine eyes for you.

TIMON: What, dost thou weep?
 Come nearer, then I love thee
 Because thou art a woman, and disclaim'st

Flinty mankind: whose eyes do never give,
But thorough lust and laughter: pity's sleeping:
Strange times you weep with laughing, not with weep-
    ing.

STEWARD: I beg of you to know me, good my Lord,
  T'accept my grief, and whil'st this poor wealth lasts,
  To entertain me as your Steward still.

TIMON: Had I a Steward
So true, so just, and now so comfortable?
It almost turns my dangerous nature wild.
Let me behold thy face: Surely, this man
Was born of woman.
Forgive my general, and exceptless rashness
You perpetual sober Gods. I do proclaim
One honest man: Mistake me not, but one:
No more I pray, and he's a Steward.
How fain would I have hated all mankind,
And thou redeem'st thyself. But all save thee,
I fell with curses.
Methinks thou art more honest now, than wise:
For, by oppressing and betraying me,
Thou might'st have sooner got another service:
For many so arrive at second Masters,
Upon their first Lord's neck. But tell me true,
(For I must ever doubt, though ne're so sure)
Is not thy kindness subtle, covetous,
If not a usuring kindness, and as rich men deal gifts,
Expecting in return twenty for one?

STEWARD: No my most worthy Master, in whose breast
  Doubt, and suspect (alas) are plac'd too late:
  You should have fear'd false times, when you did feast.
  Suspect still comes, where an estate is least.
  That which I show, Heaven knows, is merely love,

Duty, and zeal, to your unmatched mind;
Care of your food and living, and believe it,
My most honour'd Lord,
For any benefit that points to me,
Either in hope, or present, I'd exchange
For this one wish, that you had power and wealth
To requite me, by making rich yourself.

TIMON: Look thee, 'tis so: thou singly honest man,
Here take: the Gods out of my misery
Has sent thee treasure. Go, live rich and happy.
But thus condition'd: Thou shalt build from men:
Hate all, curse all, show charity to none,
But let the famish'd flesh slide from the bone,
E'er thou relieve the Beggar. Give to dogs
What thou deniest to men. Let prisons swallow 'em,
Debts wither 'em to nothing, be men like blasted woods
And may diseases lick up their false bloods,
And so farewell, and thrive.

STEWARD: O let me stay, and comfort you, my Master.

TIMON: If thou hat'st curses
Stay not: fly, whil'st thou art blessed and free:
Ne'er see thou man, and let me ne'er see thee.

Exeunt.

V. I

Enter Poet, and Painter.

PAINTER: As I took note of the place, it cannot be far
where he abides.

POET: What's to be thought of him?
Does the rumour hold for true,
That he's so full of gold?

PAINTER: Certain.

Alcibiades reports it: Phrynia and Timandra
Had gold of him. He likewise enrich'd
Poor straggling soldiers, with great quantity.
'Tis said, he gave unto his Steward
A mighty sum.

POET: Then this breaking of his,
Has been but a try for his friends?

PAINTER: Nothing else:
You shall see him a palm in Athens again,
And flourish with the highest:
Therefore, 'tis not amiss, we tender our loves
To him, in this suppos'd distress of his:
It will show honestly in us,
And is very likely, to load our purposes
With what they travail for,
If it be a just and true report, that goes
Of his having.

POET: What have you now
To present unto him?

PAINTER: Nothing at this time
But my visitation: only I will promise him
An excellent piece.

POET: I must serve him so too:
Tell him of an intent that's coming toward him.

PAINTER: Good as the best.
Promising, is the very air o'th'time;
It opens the eyes of Expectation.
Performance, is ever the duller for his act,
And but in the plainer and simpler kind of people,
The deed of saying is quite out of use.
To promise, is most courtly and fashionable;
Performance, is a kind of will or testament
Which argues a great sickness in his judgement

That makes it.
Enter Timon from his Cave.

TIMON: Excellent workman,
Thou canst not paint a man so bad
As is thyself.

POET: I am thinking
What I shall say I have provided for him:
It must be a personating of himself:
A Satire against the softness of prosperity,
With a discovery of the infinite flatteries
That follow youth and opulency.

TIMON: Must thou needs
Stand for a villain in thine own work?
Wilt thou whip thine own faults in other men?
Do so, I have gold for thee.

POET: Nay let's seek him.
Then do we sin against our own estate,
When we may profit meet, and come too late.

PAINTER: True:
When the day serves before black-corner'd night;
Find what thou want'st, by free and offer'd light.
Come.

TIMON: I'll meet you at the turn:
What a God's gold, that he is worshipp'd
In a baser Temple, than where swine feed?
'Tis thou that rigg'st the bark, and plough'st the foam,
Settlest admired reverence in a slave,
To thee be worshipp'd, and thy Saints for aye:
Be crown'd with plagues, that thee alone obey.
Fit I meet them.

POET: Hail worthy Timon.

PAINTER: Our late noble Master.

TIMON: Have I once liv'd

To see two honest men?

POET: Sir:
Having often of your open bounty tasted,
Hearing you were retir'd, your friends fallen off,
Whose thankless natures (O abhorred spirits),
Not all the whips of Heaven, are large enough.
What, to you,
Whose star-like nobleness gave life and influence
To their whole being? I am rapt, and cannot cover
The monstrous bulk of this ingratitude
With any size of words.

TIMON: Let it go,
Naked men may see't the better:
You that are honest, by being what you are,
Make them best seen, and known.

PAINTER: He, and myself
Have travail'd in the great shower of your gifts,
And sweetly felt it.

TIMON: Ay, you are honest men.

PAINTER: We are hither come
To offer you our service.

TIMON: Most honest men:
Why how shall I requite you?
Can you eat roots, and drink cold water, no?

BOTH: What we can do,
We'll do to do you service.

TIMON: Y'are honest men,
Y'have heard that I have gold,
I am sure you have, speak truth, y'are honest men.

PAINTER: So it is said my noble Lord, but therefore
Came not my Friend, nor I.

TIMON: Good honest men: Thou draw'st a counterfeit
Best in all Athens, th'art indeed the best,

D

Thou counterfeit'st most lively.

PAINTER: So, so, my Lord.

TIMON: E'en so sir as I say. And for thy fiction,
Why thy verse swells with stuff so fine and smooth,
That thou art even natural in thine Art.
But for all this (my honest natur'd friends)
I must needs say you have a little fault,
Marry 'tis not monstrous in you, neither wish I
You take much pains to mend.

BOTH: Beseech your Honour
To make it known to us.

TIMON: You'll take it ill.

BOTH: Most thankfully, my Lord.

TIMON: Will you indeed?

BOTH: Doubt it not worthy Lord.

TIMON: There's never a one of you but trusts a knave,
That mightily deceives you.

BOTH: Do we, my Lord?

TIMON: Ay, and you hear him cog,
See him dissemble,
Know his gross patchery, love him, feed him,
Keep in your bosom, yet remain assur'd
That he's a made-up-villain.

PAINTER: I know none such, my Lord.

POET: Nor I.

TIMON: Look you,
I love you well, I'll give you gold
Rid me these villains from your companies;
Hang them, or stab them, drown them in a draught,
Confound them by some course, and come to me,
I'll give you gold enough.

BOTH: Name them my Lord, let's know them.

TIMON: You that way, and you this:

But two in company:
Each man apart, all single, and alone,
Yet an arch villain keeps him company:
If where thou art, two villains shall not be,
Come not near him. If thou would'st not reside
But where one villain is, then him abandon.
Hence, pack, there's gold, you came for gold ye slaves:
You have work for me; there's payment, hence,
You are an Alchemist, make gold of that:
Out rascal dogs.

Exeunt.
Enter Steward, and two Senators.

STEWARD: It is vain that you would speak with Timon:
For he is set so only to himself,
That nothing but himself, which looks like man,
Is friendly with him.

1 SENATOR: Bring us to his Cave.
It is our part and promise to th'Athenians
To speak with Timon.

2 SENATOR: At all times alike
Men are not still the same: 'twas time and griefs
That fram'd him thus. Time with his fairer hand,
Offering the fortunes of his former days,
The former man may make him: bring us to him
And chanc'd it as it may.

STEWARD: Here is his cave:
Peace and content be here. Lord Timon, Timon,
Look out, and speak to friends: Th'Athenians
By two of their most reverend Senate greet thee:
Speak to them noble Timon.

Enter Timon out of his Cave.

TIMON: Thou Sun that comforts burn,
Speak and be hang'd:

For each true word, a blister, and each false
Be as a cantherizing to the root o'th'tongue,
Consuming it with speaking.

1 SENATOR: Worthy Timon.

TIMON: Of none but such as you,
And you of Timon.

1 SENATOR: The Senators of Athens, greet thee Timon.

TIMON: I thank them,
And would send them back the plague,
Could I but catch it for them.

1 SENATOR: O forget
What we are sorry for ourselves in thee:
The Senators, with one consent of love,
Entreat thee back to Athens, who have thought
On special dignities, which vacant lie
For thy best use and wearing.

2 SENATOR: They confess
Toward thee, forgetfulness too general gross;
Which now the public Body, which doth seldom
Play the recanter, feeling in itself
A lack of Timon's aid, hath since withall
Of it own fall, restraining aid to Timon,
And send forth us, to make their sorrowed render,
Together, with a recompence more fruitful
Than their offence can weigh down by the dram,
Ay even such heaps and sums of love and wealth,
As shall to thee blot out, what wrongs were theirs,
And write in thee the figures of their love,
Ever to read them thine.

TIMON: You witch me in it;
Surprise me to the very brink of tears;
Lend me a fool's heart, and a woman's eyes,
And I'll beweep these comforts, worthy Senators.

1 SENATOR: Therefore so please thee to return with us,
   And of our Athens, thine and ours to take
   The Captainship, thou shalt be met with thanks,
   Allowed with absolute power, and thy good name
   Live with authority: so soon we shall drive back
   Of Alcibiades th'approaches wild,
   Who like a boar too savage, doth root up
   His Country's peace.

2 SENATOR: And shakes his threat'ning sword
   Against the walls of Athens.

1 SENATOR: Therefore Timon –

TIMON: Well sir, I will: therefore I will sir thus:
   If Alcibiades kill my countrymen,
   Let Alcibiades know this of Timon,
   That Timon cares not. But if he sack fair Athens,
   And take our goodly aged men by th'beards,
   Giving our holy virgins to the stain
   Of contumelious, beastly, mad-brain'd war:
   Then let him know, and tell him Timon speaks it,
   In pity of our aged, and our youth,
   I cannot choose but tell him that I care not,
   And let him tak't at worst: For their knives care not,
   While you have throats to answer. For myself,
   There's not a whittle, in th'unruly Camp,
   But I do prize it at my love, before
   The reverend'st throat in Athens. So I leave you
   To the protection of the prosperous Gods,
   As thieves to keepers.

STEWARD: Stay not, all's in vain.

TIMON: Why I was writing of my Epitaph,
   It will be seen tomorrow. My long sickness
   Of health, and living, now begins to mend,
   And nothing brings me all things. Go, live still,

  Be Alcibiades your plague; you his,
  And last so long enough.
1 SENATOR: We speak in vain.
TIMON: But yet I love my Country, and am not
  One that rejoices in the common wrack,
  As common bruit doth put it.
1 SENATOR: That's well spoke.
TIMON: Commend me to my loving countrymen.
1 SENATOR: These words become your lips as they pass
  thorough them.
2 SENATOR: And enter in our ears, like great triumphers
  In their applauding gates.
TIMON: Commend me to them,
  And tell them, that to ease them of their griefs,
  Their fears of hostile strokes, their aches, losses,
  Their pangs of love, with other incident throes
  That Nature's fragile vessel doth sustain
  In life's uncertain voyage, I will some kindness do them,
  I'll teach them to prevent wild Alcibiades' wrath.
1 SENATOR: I like this well, he will return again.
TIMON: I have a tree which grows here in my close,
  That mine own use invites me to cut down,
  And shortly must I fell it. Tell my Friends,
  Tell Athens, in the sequence of degree,
  From high to low throughout, that who so please
  To stop affliction, let him take his haste;
  Come hither ere my tree hath felt the axe,
  And hang himself. I pray you do my greeting.
STEWARD: Trouble him no further, thus you still shall
  Find him.
TIMON: Come not to me again, but say to Athens,
  Timon hath made his everlasting mansion
  Upon the beached verge of the salt flood,

Who once a day with his embossed froth
The turbulent surge shall cover; thither come,
And let my gravestone be your Oracle:
Lips, let four words go by, and language end:
What is amiss, Plague and Infection mend.
Graves only be men's works, and Death their gain;
Sun, hide thy beams, Timon hath done his reign.

Exit Timon.

1 SENATOR: His discontents are unremovably coupled to
nature.

2 SENATOR: Our hope in him is dead: let us return,
And strain what other means is left unto us
In our dear peril.

1 SENATOR: It requires swift foot.

Exeunt.

V.2

Enter two other Senators, with a Messenger.

1 SENATOR: Thou hast painfully discover'd: are his files
As full as they report?

MESSENGER: I have spoke the least.
Besides his expedition promises present approach.

2 SENATOR: We stand much hazard, if they bring not
Timon.

MESSENGER: I met a courier, one mine ancient Friend,
Whom though in general part we were oppos'd,
Yet our old love made a particular force,
And made us speak like friends. This man was riding
From Alcibiades to Timon's Cave,
With letters of entreaty, which imported
His fellowship i'th'cause against your City,
In part for his sake mov'd.

Enter the other Senators.

1 SENATOR: Here come our Brothers.

3 SENATOR: No talk of Timon, nothing of him expect,
The Enemy's drum is heard, and fearful scouring
Doth choke the air with dust: In, and prepare,
Ours is the fall I fear, our foes the snare.

Exeunt.

V. 3

Enter a Soldier in the Woods, seeking Timon.

SOLDIER: By all description this should be the place.
Who's here? Speak hoa. No answer? What is this?
Timon is dead, who hath out-stretch'd his span,
Some beast read this; There does not live a Man.
Dead sure, and this his grave, what's on this tomb,
I cannot read: the character I'll take with wax,
Our Captain hath in every figure skill;
An ag'd interpreter, though young in days;
Before proud Athens he's set down by this,
Whose fall the mark of his ambition is.

Exit.

V. 4

*Trumpets sound. Enter Alcibiades with his Powers
before Athens.*

ALCIBIADES: Sound to this coward, and lascivious Town,
Our terrible approach.

Sounds a Parley.

The Senators appear upon the walls.

Till now you have gone on, and fill'd the time
With all licentious measure, making your wills

The scope of Justice. Till now, myself and such
As slept within the shadow of your power
Have wander'd with our travers'd arms, and breath'd
Our sufferance vainly: Now the time is flush,
When crouching marrow in the bearer strong
Cries (of itself) no more: Now breathless wrong,
Shall sit and pant in your great Chairs of ease,
And pursy Insolence shall break his wind
With fear and horrid flight.

1 SENATOR: Noble, and young;
When thy first griefs were but a mere conceit,
E'er thou had'st power, or we had cause of fear,
We sent to thee, to give thy rages balm,
To wipe out our ingratitude, with loves
Above their quantity.

2 SENATOR: So did we woo
Transformed Timon, to our City's love
By humble message, and by promised means:
We were not all unkind, nor all deserve
The common stroke of war.

1 SENATOR: These walls of ours,
Were not erected by th eir hands, fromwhom
You have receiv'd your grief: Nor are they such,
That these great towers, trophies, and schools should fall
For private faults in them.

2 SENATOR: Nor are they living
Who were the motives that you first went out,
Shame that they wanted, cunning in excess
Hath broke their hearts. March, noble Lord,
Into our City with thy banners spread,
By decimation and a tithed death;
If thy revenges hunger for that food
Which Nature loathes, take thou the destin'd tenth,

And by the hazard of the spotted die,
Let die the spotted.

1 SENATOR: All have not offended:
For those that were, it is not square to take
On those that are, revenge: Crimes, like lands
Are not inherited, then dear countryman,
Bring in thy ranks, but leave without thy rage,
Spare thy Athenian cradle, and those kin
Which in the bluster of thy wrath must fall
With those that have offended, like a shepherd,
Approach the fold, and cull th'infected forth,
But kill not altogether.

2 SENATOR: What thou wilt,
Thou rather shalt inforce it with thy smile,
Than hew to't, with thy sword.

1 SENATOR: Set but thy foot
Against our rampir'd gates, and they shall ope:
So thou wilt send thy gentle heart before,
To say thou't enter friendly.

2 SENATOR: Throw thy glove,
Or any token of thine honour else,
That thou wilt use the wars as thy redress,
And not as our confusion: All thy powers
Shall make their harbour in our Town, till we
Have seal'd thy full desire.

ALCIBIADES: Then there's my glove,
Defend and open your uncharged ports,
Those enemies of Timon's, and mine own
Whom you yourselves shall set out for reproof,
Fall and no more; and to attone your fears
With my more noble meaning, not a man
Shall pass his quarter, or offend the stream
Of regular justice in your City's bounds,

But shall be remedied to your public Laws
At heaviest answer.

BOTH: 'Tis most nobly spoken.

ALCIBIADES: Descend, and keep your words.

Enter a Messenger.

MESSENGER: My Noble General, Timon is dead,
Entomb'd upon the very hem o'th'Sea,
And on his gravestone, this insculpture which
With wax I brought away: whose soft impression
Interprets for my poor ignorance.

Alcibiades reads the Epitaph.

Here lies a wretched corse, of wretched soul bereft,
Seek not my name: A plague consume you, wicked caitiffs left:
Here lie I Timon, who alive, all living men did hate,
Pass by, and curse thy fill, but pass and stay not here thy gait.
These well express in thee thy latter spirits:
Though thou abhorr'd'st in us our human griefs,
Scorn'd'st our brains' flow, and those our droplets, which
From niggard Nature fall; yet rich conceit
Taught thee to make vast Neptune weep for aye
On thy low grave, on faults forgiven. Dead
Is noble Timon, of whose memory
Hereafter more. Bring me into your City,
And I will use the olive, with my sword:
Make war breed peace; make peace stint war, make each
Prescribe to other, as each other's leech.
Let our drums strike.

Exeunt.

NOTES

References are to the page and line of this edition.
A full page contains 33 lines.

The Actors' Names: This list appears at the end of the   P. 24
text in the Folio.

But . . . matches: what's peculiar in that? Is there any- P. 25
thing so strange that it cannot be paralleled in his-   LL. 8–9
tory?

Magic of bounty: i.e. a bountiful man is like a magi- P. 25 L. 10
cian who conjures up spirits.

touch the estimate: pay the price.   P. 25 L. 22

current . . . chafes: swirls back each time it meets an P. 26
obstacle.   LL. 5–6

heels . . . presentment: directly I have presented the P. 26 L. 8
first copy. A book which was dedicated to a distinguished patron was not offered for sale to the public
until the patron had accepted his copy.

How . . . standing: you have admirably represented P. 26
the gracious appearance of Timon.   LL. 13–14

tutors Nature: teaches Nature, i.e. is better than the P. 26 L. 21
real thing.

beneath world: i.e. the Earth is beneath Heaven.   P. 26 L. 29

My free . . . behind: This poet (as becomes a poet in P. 26 L. 30–
the age of Metaphysical Poetry) cannot make a   P. 27 L. 2
plain statement but must use a variety of images.
His general meaning is that there is no malice or
satire in his work; it is all plain and smooth – like the
surface of wax that has been melted and gone hard
and smooth. At P. 27 L. 1 he varies the image to the
straight course of a bullet and the direct flight of
an eagle which leaves no trace (*tract*) behind.

tender down: lay on the ground as offerings.   P. 27 L. 7

P. 27   *his large . . . hearts:* his great wealth subdues and
LL. 8–11   makes his own (*properties*) all kinds of men, so that
they love him and crowd his house (*tendance*).

P. 27 L. 11   *glass-fac'd:* reflecting the whim of the flattered.

P. 27 L. 20   *rank'd . . . deserts:* shows all kinds of men in rows
(*ranks*).

P. 27 L. 22   *propagate . . . states:* increase his fortune.

P. 27 L. 23   *Sovereign Lady:* Queen, i.e. Fortune.

P. 27   *whose . . . rivals:* whose present good fortune turns
LL. 26–7   his rivals into his slaves.

P. 27 L. 28   *'Tis conceiv'd, to scope:* the idea is, to represent.

P. 27 L. 33   *condition:* art, i.e., we artists are well able to express
the climbing fortunes of Timon.

P. 28 L. 3   *better . . . value:* who are wealthier than he.

P. 28 L. 6   *sacred . . . stirrup:* It was a mark of respect to hold the
stirrup of a great man as he mounted his horse.
Timon's followers regard this menial service as
almost sacred.

P. 28 LL. 6–7   *through him . . . air:* pretend that they breathe by his
permission.

P. 28 L. 19   *foot . . . head:* i.e. men can change places.

P. 28 L. 24   *talents:* the largest monetary unit of antiquity, which
cannot be satisfactorily expressed in modern equiva-
lent; here used for 'a vast sum', 'a thousand'.

P. 28 L. 30   *of that feather:* that kind of bird.

P. 29 L. I   *ever binds:* makes him your debtor for ever.

P. 29 L. 20   *one . . . trencher:* a serving man who waits at table.
trencher: wooden platter.

P. 29 L. 24   *a' th' youngest:* almost too young.

P. 30 L. 3   *precedent:* former, i.e. felt in youth.

P. 30 L. 17   *bond in men:* i.e. I am bound to help a faithful servant.

P. 30   *That state . . . you:* I shall owe you my fortunes for
LL. 25–6   ever.

suffered under-praise : has not been sufficiently praised – but the jeweller thinks at first he means under-praised, disparaged. P. 31 L. 11

will . . . chid : i.e. now look out for abuse. P. 31 L. 26

Till . . . honest : you won't get a 'good morrow' from me till I turn gentle, which will be when you become a dog, and these men turn honest. P. 31 LL. 31-3

Right . . . Law : if it's a capital offence to do nothing – for since no honest Athenian has any brains, they can't be knocked out. P. 32 L. 14

innocence : simplicity, i.e. it's a childish piece of work. P. 32 L. 16

That . . . Lord : because I lack the hot temper of a great man; editors, however, usually emend 'angry wit' to 'angry wish', 'empty wit' etc. P. 33 L. 24

Traffic . . . thee : may trade ruin you. P. 33 L. 27

All of companionship : all firm friends. P. 33 L. 33

sights : i.e. what you have to show me. P. 34 L. 4

aches : pronounced as a dissyllable, like 'h's'. P. 34 L. 7

That . . . still : there's always time for that. P. 34 L. 21

use of quittance : normal rate of exchange. P. 35 L. 12

Banquet : light refreshments, not a formal feast; but banquets at this time were very elaborate. P. 35 L. 19

faults . . . fair : the faults of generosity of rich men are really good deeds. P. 36 L. 6

ceremony : Timon here rebukes his guests for their formal gestures of politeness. P. 36 L. 8

confess'd . . . hang'd : an allusion to the proverb 'confess and be hanged.' P. 36 L. 15

Ira . . . est : anger is a short fit of madness. P. 36 L. 22

all . . . too : what makes it so mad is that he encourages them to prey on him. P. 37 LL. 2-3

without knives : It was usual for a guest to bring with him his knife and spoon. P. 37 L. 5

P. 37 L.9   *divided draught*: a cup shared by two friends.

P. 37   *spy ... notes*: i.e. see your throat occupied in drinking
LL. 11-12   – and take the opportunity to cut it.

P. 37 L. 14   *in heart*: from the bottom of my heart.

P. 38 L. 14   *use our hearts*: test our true feelings.

P. 38 L. 30   *properer*: more one's own.

P. 38 L. 33–   *Oh joys ... born*: i.e. I am so overcome by emotion
P. 39 L. 1   that my joy turns to tears.

P. 39 LL. 1-2 *hold out water*: refrain from tears.

P. 39 L. 6   *babe*: A tear was sometimes called 'a baby in the eye.'

P. 39 L. 20   *Cupid*: When uninvited maskers wished to attend a
               party, it was customary for them to announce their
               coming by sending in a messenger, symbolically
               costumed, to make an appropriate speech. See *Romeo
               and Juliet*, I. 4, 1-3. Masques were especially popular
               in the reigns of James I and Charles I; they were
               acted by amateurs of noble or gentle birth.

P. 39 L. 31   *sweep of vanity*: crowd of over-dressed women.

P. 39 L. 33–   *Like ... Envy*: this wild display (*glory*) is as mad as an
P. 40 L. 5   extravagant feast (*pomp*) compared with a philoso-
               pher's fare (*oil and roots*). We make fools of ourselves
               in our entertainments and waste flattery when we
               praise excessively (*drink up*) those men whom later
               we shall vomit up through sheer spite and envy.

P. 40 L. 21   *own device*: masque which I myself composed.

P. 41 LL. 4-5 *'Tis ... mind*: it is a pity that a man cannot see that
               his generosity will soon cause him wretchedness.

P. 41 L. 30   *trapp'd*: with its harness studded with silver.

P. 41   *presents ... entertained*: be treated with great honour
LL. 31-2   – and those bring them be rewarded.

P. 42 L. 18   *put ... books*: in their debt.

P. 43 L. 4   *call to*: call on – when I am in need.

P. 43 L. 23   *serving of becks*: obsequious bows.

give . . . shortly: you'll find yourself in a pillory with P. 44 L. 1
your faults set out on a placard.

foals . . . horses: i.e. in return for my gift of one horse P. 44
Timon gives me several.   LL. 21–2

Porter: whose duty was to keep the rogues out, not to P. 44 L. 22
invite them in.

Commend . . . hand: i.e. when Timon takes off his cap P. 45 LL. 3–4
and makes polite remarks about me.

fracted dates: broken promises of repayment.   P. 45 L. 7

When . . . Phoenix: when every borrowed feather, P. 45
which now makes Timon as bright as the phoenix, LL. 15–17
has been repaid, he will be as naked as a newly
hatched gull. The gull is used as the type of a silly
bird, the phoenix as something rare, strange, and
magnificent.

have the dates in: date when each is due.   P. 45 L. 21

discharg'd: sent away with what we have come for.   P. 46 L. 11

succession . . . days: from one day to the next.   P. 46 L. 22

with . . . suit: you show your noble nature by repay- P. 46 L. 25
ing.

due on forfeiture: on penalty of forfeiting the security. P. 47 L. 2

out-runst grace: you go faster than goodness.   P. 48 L. 33

Mistress: like Mistress Overdone in *Measure for* P. 49 L. 11
Measure, she keeps a bawdy house.

artificial one: i.e. the philosopher's stone for which P. 49 L. 23
alchemists were still researching.

I . . . philosophers: i.e. lovers (*who are mad*) elder P. 50 LL. 1–2
brothers (*who are extravagant*), women (*who are fickle*)
are not the only fools, but philosophers also sometimes.

rated . . . means: reckoned my spending according to P. 50 LL. 8–9
my means.

Perchance . . . yourself: you may have occasionally P. 50
raised the matter when I was unwilling to hear you, LL. 13–16
and you have used that reluctance to excuse yourself.

P. 51 LL. 2-3 *defend . . . reck'ning*: how shall we meet the debts of the near future, and the final reckoning?

P. 51 LL. 16-17 *retir'd . . . flow*: A much debated phrase. As it stands it means, 'I have sat beside the running tap and there wept' – which seems hardly in keeping with the Steward's nature or behaviour. Editors emend variously, for *cock* reading 'couch', 'cot', 'compt', etc.

P. 51 L. 27 *Feast . . . lost*: a friend won by feasting is soon lost.

P. 51 L. 33 *secure thy heart*: don't worry.

P. 52 L. 5 *Assurance . . . thoughts*: may your thoughts prove true.

P. 52 L. 27 *general way*: likely means.

P. 52 L. 28 *use . . . name*: i.e. I have written letters in your name.

P. 53 LL. 14-15 *And Nature . . . heavy*: i.e. as they grow old, they become mean.

P 55 L. 31-2 *unto . . . in him*: has been made honourable by eating his dinner.

P. 56 L. 5 *prolong his hour*: may he die slowly.

P. 56 L. 19 *urg'd extremely*: requested most urgently.

P. 57 L. 31 *conceive the fairest*: think most kindly.

P. 58 L. 15 *dips . . . dish*: It was the custom of friends to sit together, four at a table, helping themselves from one common dish.

P. 60 LL. 9-11 *the devil . . . clear*: i.e. the devil made a mistake when he made men crafty; he thwarted (*crossed*) himself; but yet men in the end will justify him by their villainies. This Lord tries to make out that he is acting honourably when he commits a foul deed; he uses the example of honourable men to justify his own wickedness.

P. 60 L. 18 *wards*: lit., the bars inside a lock which fit the notches in a key. The doors which were once open to all comers must now be locked to keep out Timon's creditors.

You . . . recoverable : i.e. the course of an extravagant man is like the sun, full of sunshine in his prosperity but showing little in his poverty; but the prodigal's winter has no return of summer. P. 61 LL. 15–16

in a cloud : in a huff. P. 62 L. 17

make . . . Gods : go to heaven with a clear conscience. P. 63 L. 19

Put . . . now : i.e. now's our chance. P. 63 L. 29

unnoted : unobserved, i.e. calm. P. 65 L. 27

behoove his anger : become his anger, i.e. though angry he was self-controlled. P. 65 L. 28

manslaughter . . . valour : to make manslaughter legal and quarrelling a necessary part of valour. P. 66 LL. 3–4

prefer . . . danger : i.e. the valiant man should never take his injuries to heart lest he fall into danger. P. 66 LL. 11–12

To . . . bear : it is valour to endure injury rather than to revenge it. P. 66 L. 17

If . . . Abroad : if it is so brave to endure injuries, why should we soldiers fight abroad? P. 66 LL. 23–5

bearing carry it : if endurance is preferable. P. 66 L. 26

But . . . just : but killing in self-defence is regarded as just by merciful men. P. 66 L. 33

sin : i.e. drunkenness. P. 67 L. 14

Though . . . none : though his valour might be considered to have paid in full for his offence. P. 67 LL. 24–5

good returns : future good behaviour. P. 67 L. 29

know : recognize my claims on you. P. 68 L. 4

Now . . . you : may you live so long that you become living skeletons whom no one will care to look at. P. 68 LL. 23–5

lay for hearts : strike to the heart. P. 69 L. 2

Soldiers . . . Gods : i.e. should revenge as quickly. P. 69 L. 4

near occasions : important affairs. P. 69 L. 16

fare . . . sound : care to listen to the harsh notes of the trumpet. P. 70 L. 10

P. 70 L. 25   *All . . . dishes:* i.e. a full dinner, not just refreshments.

P. 71 L. 11   *City Feast:* a formal banquet when every guest is on his best behaviour.

P. 71 L. 22   *fees:* the meaning is doubtful.

P. 71 L. 23   *leg:* some editors emend to *lag:* rabble.

P. 72 L. 6   *Fools of Fortune:* fools who follow Fortune (and desert when things go wrong).

P. 72 L. 7   *Cap and knee slaves:* fawning beggars.

P. 72 L. 7   *minute jacks:* The jack is the figure on an ornamental clock which strikes the hours – used as an image for a senseless flatterer.

P. 72   *Of man . . . o'er:* may every disease suffered by man
LL. 8–9   and beast cover you with blotches.

P. 73 L. 7   *general filths:* common harlots.

P. 73 L. 9   *hold fast:* don't pay your debts.

P. 73 L. 11   *Bound servants:* apprentices bound by solemn agreement to serve their masters faithfully.

P. 73 L. 19   *Mysteries:* skilled trades – in which a spirit of brotherhood was strong.

P. 73 L. 21   *confounding contraries:* destructive opposites.

P. 74 L. 23   *take . . . arm:* support him in his troubles.

P. 75 L. 26   *painted . . . varnish'd:* outwardly bright and glossy.

P. 76 L. 5   *that . . . it:* i.e. money to buy necessities.

P. 76 L. 12   *Sister's Orb:* i.e. the Moon.

P. 76   *Twinn'd . . . lesser:* give to twin brothers who lived
LL. 13–16   in the same womb such diverse fortunes that the greater may scorn the lesser.

P. 76   *Not . . . Nature:* human nature, liable to every kind
LL. 16–18   of disease, can only endure great wealth by despising nature.

P. 76 L. 20   *contempt hereditary:* inherit contempt as natural to their position.

the Pastor ... leave: this is the Folio reading. It has P. 76
been emended to 'the pasture lard (make fat) the LL. 22–3
rother's (horned beast's) sides.'

idle votarist: one who utters frivolous prayers. P. 77 L. 7

Pluck ... heads: cause strong men to be smothered in P. 77 L. 13
their beds.

cast ... gorge: vomit. P. 77 L. 21

embalms ... day: makes as sweet smelling as April P. 77
flowers. LL. 21–2

puts odds: makes quarrels. P. 77 L. 23

quick: living, because gold can accomplish so much. P. 77 L. 27

Athenian minion: darling of Athens. P. 79 L. 5

Voic'd so regardfully: praised so honourably. P. 79 L. 6

tubs and baths: The treatment for venereal disease was P. 79 L. 11
a course of hot baths.

fubfast: usually emended to *tubfast:* sweating treat- P. 79 L. 12
ment.

planetary plague: plague sent by a planet, visitation of P. 80 L. 6
divine wrath.

window barn: The Folio reads 'through the window P. 80 L. 12
Barne bore at.' Dr Johnson emended to 'window-
bars'. The passage then means 'fascinate men's eyes
as they are exposed through the openings in the
bosom of the dress.' When this play was written it
was fashionable for unmarried women to bare their
breasts.

bastard ... pronounced: about which the Oracle has P. 80
made some riddling prophecy, as, e.g. the Oracle L. 18–19
foretold that the babe Oedipus would kill his father
and marry his mother and was therefore cast out to
die.

Swear ... objects: swear not to spare objects of pity. P. 80 L. 20

conditions: natural wickedness. P. 81 L. 6

yet ... contrary: The phrase is much disputed but P. 81
probably means 'may you in your turn suffer from LL. 10–11

venereal disease for six months'. Among the more
devastating results of the disease in former times
were rotting of the flesh, loss of hair, ulcers, loss of
the nose, softening of the bones – over which Timon
gloats on P. 81 L. 19.

P. 81   *thatch . . . dead :* i.e. cover your bald heads with hair
LL. 11–12   taken from the dead. Shakespeare seems to have been
              particularly disgusted by the wig-maker's custom of
              obtaining human hair from corpses: see *Merchant of
              Venice* III. 2. 92–96 and Sonnet 68.

P. 81 L. 16   *pox of wrinkles :* to hell with wrinkles – for paint will
              hide them.

P. 81 L. 21   *mar . . . spurring :* because of sore heels.

P. 81   *that . . . weal :* of that man who in following his own
LL. 27–8   good does not stink like the rest.

P. 81 L. 30   *unscarr'd braggarts :* unwounded boasters.

P. 82 L. 2   *ditches . . . all :* i.e. when dead may you be thrown into
              a ditch (like a dead dog).

P. 82 L. 23   *eyeless . . . worm :* 'blind worm', actually a legless
              lizard common in the English countryside.

P. 82 L. 32   *marbled mansion :* sky mottled with clouds.

P. 83 L. 11   *infected :* i.e. you are not a genuine melancholic; you
              have merely caught the disease.

P. 83 L. 13   *future :* i.e. because your future life is likely to be so
              different from your past. Some editors emend to
              'fortune'.

P. 83 L. 16   *diseas'd perfumes :* their diseased scented whores.

P. 83 L. 18   *cunning of a Carper :* expert knowledge of a true cynic.

P. 84   *willing . . . content :* the man who is voluntarily mel-
LL. 25–30   ancholic lives longer than the wealthy man with his
              uncertainties and gets his reward sooner (*is crown'd*).
              The wealthy man is never satisfied, never full; the
              melancholy man always has what he desires (*at high
              wish*). The rich man has no content because he is a
              distracted and most wretched being; but the man
              who is in the lowest condition is content.

passive drugs : unresisting drudges.   P. 85 L. 4

confectionary : the room in a great house where the   P. 85 L. 10
sweatmeats and preserves were made and stored.
Timon answers Apemantus's sneer by saying that if
Apemantus had enjoyed similar great wealth he
would have grossly misused it; but since he was born
a beggar he has no justification for cursing the ingratitude of men.

Poor . . . hereditary : born a poor beggar.   P. 85 L. 24

have to Athens : wish to happen to.   P. 86 L. 8

medlar : a fruit resembling a crab apple, eaten when it   P. 86 L. 26
has begun to go rotten.

unthrift . . . means : a spendthrift who was still loved   P. 86
after his money was gone.   LL. 32–3

german : related to. It was believed that a leopard was   P. 87 L. 28
the result of the mating of a lion and a 'pard'.

spots : crimes – with a pun on the leopard's spots.   P. 87 L. 29

jurors . . . life : would condemn you to death.   P. 87 L. 29

cap : i.e. the Fool's cockscomb.   P. 88 L. 17

quit : have paid my debt.   P. 90 L. 1

limited professions : restricted, governed by rules of   P. 91 L. 6
admission.

protest to do't : claim that you are a villain.   P. 91 L. 12

Live . . . thieving : I'll prove to you that there are   P. 91 L. 13
plenty of other examples of thieves.

How . . . enemies : how seldom nowadays is it   P. 92
fashionable for a man to obey the command to love   LL. 12–13
his enemies.

Suspect . . . least : only poor men are suspicious.   P. 93 L. 32

from men : far away from men.   P. 94 L. 11

load . . . for : brings us the reward we were labouring   P. 95
for.   LL. 14–15

Promising . . . makes it : i.e. nowadays everyone   P. 95 L. 26–
promises, but only a fool fulfills his promises.   P. 96 L. 1

P. 95 L. 30   *deed of saying:* i.e. to follow words with actions.

P. 96 L. 23   *at the turn:* when you turn round. The Poet and the Painter have been walking up and down at the front of the main stage while Timon lurks at the rear. At 'Fit I meet them', Timon comes forward.

P. 96 L. 27   *Settlest . . . slave:* causes a slave to wonder excessively.

P. 97 L. 32   *counterfeit:* portrait – but with the double meaning of 'fake'.

P. 98 L. 5   *natural:* lifelike – but with the double meaning of 'born fool'.

P. 99   *Each man . . . company:* each of you when alone is
LL. 2–3   accompanied by a villain, i.e. you are both complete knaves.

P. 100 L. 23   *sorrowed render:* sorrowful confession.

P. 100 L. 25   *dram:* lit., the sixteenth part of an ounce; i.e. the recompence shall far outweigh the injury.

P. 101 L. 22   *tak't at worst:* do his worst.

P. 101 L. 33   *nothing . . . things:* i.e. when I am no more I shall be part of the universe.

P. 102 L. 21   *have a tree:* see Introduction P. 18.

P. 102 L. 24   *sequence of degree:* order of rank.

P. 102   *still . . . him:* i.e. he's always like this.
LL. 29–30

P. 103 L. 1   *who:* i.e. the flood.

P. 103   *coupled to nature:* part of his nature.
LL. 9–10

P. 103 L. 17   *painfully discover'd:* your information is painful.

P. 104 L. 11   *outstretch'd his span:* stretched out his full span of life, i.e. died.

P. 104 L. 14   *character . . . wax:* I will take an impression of the writing (*character*) in wax.

P. 104 L. 17   *set down:* has begun the siege.

making . . . Justice: making Justice depend on your desires. — P. 104 L. 27– P. 105 L. 1

crouching marrow: strength ready for the spring. — P. 105 L. 5

decimation . . . tithed death: the selection of one man in ten to be put to death. — P. 105 L. 31

that were: that are dead. — P. 106 L. 4

Throw . . . glove: as a token of your promise. — P. 106 L. 20

seal'd: formally agreed. — P. 106 L. 25

uncharged ports: unassailed gates. — P. 106 L. 27

pass his quarter: leave his quarters. — P. 106 L. 32

the Epitaph: This Epitaph is taken verbatim from Plutarch; see Introduction P. 17. — P. 107 L. 11

use the olive: i.e. bring peace. — P. 107 L. 24

GLOSSARY

accompts : accounts
arrant : out and out
assay : attempt

balm : healing ointment
balsam : healing ointment
bark : ship
bates : diminishes
bawd : go-between
beagles : lit., small hounds, women followers
bear : carry off
botch'd : clumsily patched
breaking : bankruptcy
breathe : exercise, exert
breath'd : exercised by constant practice
broach : set flowing

caitiff : wretch
candied : covered with ice
canker : cankerworm, maggot
canon : ecclesiastical law
cashier'd : dismissed
caudle : bring a warm drink to
cauteriz'd : cauterized
chamberlain : valet
choler : anger
churl : boor
close : private garden
coffer : treasury
cog : cheat
comfortable : full of comfort
compassion : spirit of mercy
composture : manure

con : learn
conceit : imagination
confluence : crowd
contumelious : insolent
Corinth : slang for a bawdy house
corse : corpse
couch'd : lie hidden
courage : determination
course : means
crisp : curly, covered with curling clouds
cull : select
curiosity : fastidiousness

dialogue : converse with
dich : do
die : dice
disfurnish'd : leave unprovided
donation : voluntary gift
draught : privy
dropping : slouching

earnest : money given on account of the main payment
embossed : foaming
enfranchise : set free
engag'd : pledged
ensear : dry up
exceptless : which admits no exception
expedition : haste

fact : deed
fang : tear to pieces

fall: low tide
feign'd: pretended, imagined
fell: knock down
fellowship: partnership
figure: writing
figures: value
file: ranks, numbers
fitly: opportunely
flamen: priest
flush: in full bloom
fond: foolish
fractures: broken sentences
frame: appearance
fram'd: made
frankly: freely
form: design
free: generous

generation: breed
grace: favour
gramercy: many thanks
grize: step
gules: red – a heraldic term
gust: blast of wind

habit: dress
half-caps: perfunctory acknow-
   ledgements
have to: wish for
having: wealth
heaven: benefit
high-vic'd: vicious
hits: guesses
hoar: white
hoar (verb): cover with white
   blotches
hoboyes: oboes
honesty: open-handedness
humours: whims

husbandry: management
Hymen: god of marriage
Hyperion: the sun god

indifferent: so so
inferred: reported
ingeniously: frankly
interpret: give life to
it: its

keep: guard
knell: passing bell, rung at the
   moment of death
knot: gang

labouring: about to bring forth,
   on the point of
latest: last
leaf: page of a book
leech: physician
lin'd: padded
liquorish: delightful
lively: lifelike

made up: complete
mark: aim
Mars: god of war
mast: acorns
maw: stomach
meed: reward, gift
mend: increase the value
merely: entirely
mess: dinner
mettle: material
minister: rule
mistook: doubted
mo, moe: more
mockery: imitation
moral: symbolical

mountant: uplifted
muffled: with the head covered
mystery: skilled trade

Neptune: the sea god

oathable: to be believed on oath
offices: rooms
operant: powerful
oppress'd: crowded
ort: scrap

pack: be off!
page (verb): follow like a page
palm: the type of flourishing
    prosperity
passes: surpasses
patchery: knavery
pawn: pledge
pill: rob
pencill'd: painted
periods: puts an end to
pitifully: mercifully
policy: craftiness
powers: army
preferr'd: put in
pregnantly: aptly, significantly
present: immediate
prompted: reminded
proof: (of armour), impene-
    trability
pursy: fat

quillet: subtlety

rampier'd: protected by ram-
    parts
ranks: soldiers

rapt: inspired, absorbed, en-
    raptured
recanter: penitent
remotion: moving away
repair: come
repugnancy: fighting back
respectively: particularly
riot: extravagance
rout: rabble

salt: bawdy
sans: without
save: God save
scouring: scurrying
season: prepare, make ready
semblable: likeness
several: different
smooth'd: flattered
solidares: coins of little worth
something: somewhat
spangled: made sparkle
speed: prosper
sphere: world
spilth: spilling
Spittle-house: hospital for ven-
    ereal disease
square: fair, just
stand for: represent, be
stepp'd into: offended against
stint: stop
strait: strict
sufferance: hardship
sugar'd: sweet
superscription: name of the ad-
    dressee
swath: swaddling clothes
sweat: labour excessively

tapsters: barmen

thorough : through

travers'd : reversed in sign of mourning

tiring : busied, occupied

touch : test, touchstone

touch'd : tested (like gold) for purity

toward : forthcoming

towardly : willing

travail'd : laboured

trenchant : carving

trencher-friends : feast-hounds, toadies

trunk : body

unbolt : open up

uncheck'd : removed the restraints on

unclew : unwind

unctuous : fat, rich

undergo : maintain

use : make use of

verge : margin

voice : vote, support

wafts : waves

wappen'd : tired

water : (of a jewel) lustre

wears : wastes away

whittle : clasp knife

whoremaster : one who frequents whores

wink : shut the eye

witch : charm

wrack : wreck, ruin

wreakful : revengeful

The Pelican Book of English Prose

GENERAL EDITOR: KENNETH ALLOTT

This book covers in five volumes English prose from the accession of Queen Elizabeth I to the Golden Jubilee of Queen Victoria. It has been planned to suit the needs of the general reader and student. Each volume has an introduction and biographical notes, and the text is arranged under these headings: (1) The Picture of the Age; (2) The Movement of Ideas; (3) The World of Imagination, Feeling, and Comic Invention; (4) The Criticism of the Arts.

Vol. 1: Elizabethan and Jacobean Prose (1550–1620)
EDITED BY KENNETH MUIR

Sidney, Bacon, Hooker and the Elizabethan pamphleteers are fully represented, but the main emphasis falls on the dramatists, novelists, and the great Tudor translators. (A360)

Vol. 2: 17th-Century Prose (1620–1700)
EDITED BY PETER URE

Prose from Donne and Sir Thomas Browne to Dryden and Locke, with stress laid on the intellectual revolutions of the time – though the diarists, character-writers, and Restoration playwrights are not forgotten. (A 361)

Vol. 3: 18th-Century Prose (1700–1780)
EDITED BY D. W. JEFFERSON

Prose from Swift to Dr Johnson, with many extracts illustrating the first great period of the English novel. Addison, Defoe, Berkeley, Chesterfield, Goldsmith, Boswell, Hume, and Gibbon are other writers who figure importantly here. (A362)

Vol. 4: Prose of the Romantic Period
EDITED BY RAYMOND WRIGHT

Burke, Cowper, Godwin, Scott, Jane Austen, Landor, Wordsworth, Coleridge, Keats, Hazlitt, and Lamb are some of the greater names among the many from whom extracts have been chosen. (A363)

Vol. 5: Victorian Prose (1830–1880)
EDITED BY KENNETH AND MIRIAM ALLOTT

Prose from Carlyle and Dickens to Hardy, Pater, and Henry James. Mill, Newman, Ruskin, Arnold, and George Eliot are writers who select themselves, but such lesser figures as Fitzgerald, Surtees, Kilvert, Bagehot, and Samuel Butler are not neglected. (A364)